rebuilding
TRUST

rebuilding
TRUST

GUIDED THERAPY TECHNIQUES AND ACTIVITIES
to Restore Love, Trust, and Intimacy
in Your Relationship

Morgan Johnson, MA, LPC

FOREWORD BY DR. GINA SENARIGHI, PhD, CPC

ZEITGEIST · NEW YORK

Published in the United States by Zeitgeist, an imprint of Zeitgeist™, a division of Penguin Random House LLC, New York.
penguinrandomhouse.com

Zeitgeist™ is a trademark of Penguin Random House LLC

ISBN: 9780593435595
Ebook ISBN: 9780593435618

Cover art © Getty Images/matsabe; interior art © Shutterstock/donatas1205
Author photograph © by Errich Petersen
Book design by Katy Brown
Edited by Clara Song Lee

Printed in China

3 5 7 9 10 8 6 4 2

To all the clients I've had the privilege
to serve and walk alongside
as they repair and rebuild their relationships

Contents

Foreword

FOR THE LAST FIFTEEN YEARS, I've been working as a couples therapist to help clients repair broken trust. Some reach out to me after a major betrayal, while others come after years of trust erosion through relationship neglect. Despite the varying circumstances, they all show up using very similar—and familiar—dialogue rooted in blame, shock, anger, and confusion.

In the aftermath of betrayal, people often find themselves at a crossroads. Many are losing sleep, ruminating while at work, and desperate to stop the waves of emotion crashing over them. They know their relationship needs to change, but they struggle to see a vision for their future. How can they bridge this gap? How can they change the dynamic so they stop turning away from each other and start turning toward each other with compassion and vulnerability?

There is hope. Partners who want to stay together can stay together if they are willing to put in the effort. With the right tools, and exercises, they can absolutely develop the skills needed to process, reconnect, and repair their relationships. With *Rebuilding Trust* by Morgan Johnson, they now have access to these tools in a clear, organized, and easy-to-follow format.

This high-integrity guide walks partners, step-by-step, through a thoughtfully researched process of self-connection and relationship repair. It helps them move through intense emotions, resolve conflicts, re-establish security, and slowly embrace trust again. This book also empowers partners to co-create a new version of their relationship that feels stronger and better than they ever imagined.

Whether you're freshly caught in the throes of a newly disclosed betrayal, finally showing up after many years of disconnection, or somewhere in between, there is something here for everyone. I am so glad you have this book to guide you through the process of healing and repair. Morgan's wisdom, kindness, and supportive reflections will transform your relationship as you find your way back to each other again.

DR. GINA SENARIGHI, PhD, CPC

Acknowledgments

I WANT TO THANK all of the clients who have trusted me to walk alongside you. You taught me more about trust and forgiveness than any training ever could, and this project would have been impossible without all our experiences together. I'd also love to acknowledge and appreciate the endless support and uplifting I received from my incredible community of family, friends, therapist, colleagues, editors, and mentors. It will never be lost on me how privileged I am to be where I am, connected with the wonderful humans I am, with the opportunity to serve in this way.

Finally, I want to thank the experts and authors whose invaluable research, knowledge, and teachings have been critical to my own training and work as a relationship counselor and trust-recovery specialist. This book would not have been possible without the incredible work of Jean Baker Miller, Harriet Lerner, Sue Johnson, Esther Perel, bell hooks, John and Julie Gottman, Caryl Rusbult, Shirley Glass, Richard Schwartz, Stephen Porges, Dan Siegel, Deb Dana, Kimberlé Crenshaw, Emily and Amelia Nagoski, Stan Tatkin, Diane Poole Heller, Babette Rothschild, Layla Saad, and Pema Chödrön. You'll hear their voices and wisdom mentioned often, and I reference their work throughout this book.

Introduction

Things falling apart is a kind of testing and also a kind of healing.

—PEMA CHÖDRÖN, BUDDHIST TEACHER AND AUTHOR

OF ALL THE WAYS our hearts can get banged up in love relationships, betrayal is unique in its ability to rock us to the core. Few other emotional experiences inspire us to question everything we thought we knew. Since you've picked up this book, I'm assuming that you are in a place of dealing with betrayal (what I'll refer to as a *relationship norm violation*, or RNV) and are unsure about what to do or how to proceed. Whatever your role in the betrayal experience, I appreciate your strength in facing it. Perhaps you violated norms in your relationship and wish to repair it, or you are choosing to stay in a relationship post-RNV. Or you are choosing to leave. Whatever your role and feelings, you are normal and human.

If you're in the process of deciding whether to stay in a relationship or end it (what relationship scientists refer to as *relational discernment*), you might find some useful ideas here, but this book is not geared toward discernment. The tools here have been carefully adapted from exercises I use every day with clients who would like to rebuild trust or at least find out what it would take to try. Healing when trust has been smashed is hard work but it absolutely can be done. In fact, many people find that doing the work to rebuild trust brings them to a level of honesty, closeness, and intimacy they didn't know was even possible.

The Importance of Trust

Trust is vital to healthy relationships because it is foundational to the attachment and intimate behaviors needed to grow and sustain a thriving, long-term bond. The Harvard Longevity Study, the longest ongoing study in the U.S. (nearly eighty years!) has examined what makes people live happy, healthy lives. Of the huge number of factors the study looked at, it turned out there's one single thing responsible for making us live longer, be less likely to experience cardiovascular disease, heart attack, and stroke, and less likely to get dementia. That single factor: being bonded with someone we trust to have our backs.

Trusting again—or truly trusting for the first time—is something we're called to actively choose to do. And it's something that can be awfully hard if we find it difficult to even trust in ourselves. When we trust ourselves, we can release resistance to trusting others because we know that regardless of how things shake out, we'll be able to ensure good care for ourselves through self-leadership and self-care as well as by recruiting trusted others and leaning into support structures and community. Learning to be more discerning when it comes to who we choose to trust—who we allow in to support our vulnerability—in and of itself can help build self-trust.

The Questions I Get Asked Most

In my work as a trust-recovery therapist, there are certain questions I am asked time and again. Chances are, you might have some of these same questions, so let's tackle them together.

Is it wrong to consider staying with someone who has betrayed me? In our culture, we often hear things like "once a cheater always a cheater" or "fool me once, shame on you; fool me twice, shame on me." Such expressions imply that choosing to stay and try to rebuild trust is somehow foolish or weak, and therefore setting ourselves up for disaster. On the contrary, it is *anything* but weak. I have profound respect for the clients and friends who let me walk alongside as they do the brave work of trusting themselves and the people they love. Likewise, if you decide that you need to dissolve the relationship without attempting to rebuild trust, that's also not weakness—you may have very good reasons, compounded or otherwise, to make such a choice. Repair work is not ideal for every relationship, especially if abuse is a factor alongside betrayal.

Do we have to hire a couples therapist? Only you and your partner can answer that. Some readers will feel enormous benefits from reading and working through this book with their partner and won't need a therapist. Others will notice a lot of ah-ha! moments and benefits but still feel stuck or hopeless about the relationship. In that case, a trained third party can offer help and direction if issues have become too big or complex to manage on your own.

Why does therapy work, and how can the tools in this book help? Relationship therapy is successful when we can increase emotional attunement between partners. This means building enough of a felt sense of safety for everyone to be vulnerable and tuned in to each other's emotional worlds. Both Emotionally Focused Therapy and the tools in this book help increase emotional attunement by empowering partners to co-create safe spaces through conversations and bonding activities. This allows you to take healthy emotional risks and reach for each other when things are hard, as well as to reliably respond to each other in ways partners can feel on a positive and nurturing emotional level.

Can trust-recovery work really succeed? Absolutely. Well over 90 percent of the relationships who wish to stay together and who go through the trust-recovery process with me *are* able to find their way back to each other and trust again. In fact, partners frequently claim a new, deeper level of relationship satisfaction than they had before. If all partners are willing to put in the time and effort involved, we can dismantle and reassemble an old version of a relationship that doesn't serve us—without actually

Disclaimer: Who Shouldn't Use These Tools

While this book is written for a wide audience, it is not a substitute for counseling and is ideally used in conjunction with ongoing professional relationship support. At the start of relationship therapy, it is normal for things to get worse before they get better. For that reason, this book alone is not recommended in certain situations, including but not limited to:

* Abusive relationships or relationships with escalated conflict cycles that partners do not feel able to stop on their own

* When one or more partners is not adequately supported to cope with an individual issue or disorder (e.g. substance dependence, out-of-control sexual behavior, or a major untreated mood disorder such as depression or CPTSD)

* If involved partner is unwilling to discontinue violating relational norms (refuses to end or effectively boundary the relationship with affair partner)

* If partners are separated and do not have enough time or space to use the tools together

If any of these situations or other areas of concern apply, please consult with a licensed professional before engaging in any of the activities in this book.

If you're experiencing a life-threatening emergency, do not attempt to use the tools in this book. Immediately call 911, go to your nearest emergency room, or utilize these emergency resources:

* National Domestic Violence Hotline: 1 (800) 799-7233

* National Suicide Prevention Hotline: 1 (800) 273-8255

* LGBT Trevor Project Lifeline: 1 (866) 488-7386

* National Sexual Assault Hotline: 1 (800) 656-4673

* Crisis Text Line: Text "HOME" to 741741

ending the relationship and thereby terminating its valuable and enduring aspects.

What if partner(s) are reluctant to try the work of trust recovery? Let's be real. Not everyone who shows up in my office is 100 percent enthusiastic about being there. Often, one partner has expressed an ultimatum that they're unwilling to consider staying in the relationship unless they do relationship counseling together.

Perhaps reading this book isn't the first thing *you* want to be doing. If that's true, I appreciate you for choosing to take a stab at something that demonstrates a willingness to show up and a desire to trust and be trusted. Some of the tools in this book can be explored and applied individually, but others require all parties in the relationship to really show up. If you've experienced a loss of trust, you'll find this book packed with practical resources you can use both on your own and with partners to get some movement in your situation.

How long does healing take? I can't make guarantees about how long it will take to get to a point in healing that's deeply satisfying for you. Relationships I've worked with average anywhere from about eight to twelve weeks to a few years of treatment. Several factors influence the amount of time and effort necessary for healing. These include the length of time between the start of the RNV and disclosure/discovery, the quality of relationship and commitment pre-RNV, the amount of lying and gaslighting involved, the depth of the RNV (Was it a one-off or was it a full-on double life? Was there love or just lust?), individual factors pre-RNV (such as whether there were already enduring vulnerabilities, such as previous experiences of RNVs from earlier relationships), as well as cultural backgrounds.

Attachment Science 101

> I want to love you without clutching, appreciate you without judging, join you without invading, invite you without demanding, leave you without guilt, criticize you without blaming, and help you without insulting. If I can have the same from you, then we can truly meet and enrich each other. —VIRGINIA SATIR, PSYCHOTHERAPIST COMMONLY CALLED THE "MOTHER OF FAMILY THERAPY"

You may be wondering how we learn to trust in the first place. In the same way that our bodies have an immune system to protect us from threats in our physical environments, we have an *attachment system* to protect us in our relational worlds. It begins as soon as we're born and interact with other humans. If we cry for help and don't get a response, our brain encodes that experience as a threat because our bodies unconsciously know that being alone or far away from a trusted human is dangerous.

Relationship scientists describe *attachment avoidance* as discomfort with getting close to people or depending on others, whereas *attachment anxiety* is discomfort with even a little distance from other people or uncertainty about a connection. Everyone generally falls somewhere on the spectrum between low and high attachment avoidance, and low and high attachment anxiety. Depending on how our caregivers responded to us—or didn't—we develop one of the four main attachment styles.

Secure attachment. Characterized as low attachment avoidance and low attachment anxiety, this generally comes from having caregivers who met our distress with steadiness, regulation, and grounding.

Anxious attachment. Characterized as low attachment avoidance and high attachment anxiety, this generally results from having caregivers who met our distress with increased distress of their own.

Attachment Styles and Default Tendencies

ATTACHMENT STYLES	SECURE	INSECURE—ANXIOUS	INSECURE—AVOIDANT	INSECURE—DISORGANIZED
Strength-based language reframe	Adaptive; nurtured in optimal conditions	Adaptive; specialized for over-stimulation	Adaptive; specialized for under-stimulation	Adaptive; specialized for chaos/danger/ both under-/ over-stimulation
How early caregivers respond to distress emotionally	With regulation more times than not	With increased stress/reactivity; dysregulation	With dismissal, denial, and/or downplaying	With unpredictable behavior and/or violence
Common cognitions/ beliefs/enduring vulnerabilities	"I am enough" "I can trust myself alone and with others"	"I'm too much" "I can't trust myself"	"I'm not enough" "I can't trust others"	"I'm both too much and not enough" "Others are scary. So is being by myself"
Common relationship tendencies when feeling overwhelmed	Self-soothe and co-regulate	Pursue/ move toward	Shut down/ withdraw/ move away	Mix of pursue and withdraw moves
Default boundary preferences	Interdependent	Prefers other-dependence	Prefers self-dependence	Fearful of self-dependence and other-dependence
Emotional processing preferences	"I can get closeness and space when I need either"	"I need others to get calm" (interpersonal process)	"I need space to calm myself" (internal process)	"I simultaneously crave distance and closeness"

Avoidant attachment. Characterized as high attachment avoidance and low attachment anxiety, this generally results from having caregivers who met our distress by dismissing, downplaying, demeaning, or ignoring it altogether.

Disorganized attachment. Characterized as high attachment avoidance and high attachment anxiety, this generally results from having caregivers who sometimes met our distress with increased distress *and at other times* met our distress with dismissal and avoidance—usually things felt scary and/or unpredictable. Another cause may be having one caregiver who met our distress in a fundamentally opposite way from another caregiver so that we experienced multiple kinds of responses.

Fortunately, even if your caregivers failed to show up as consistently as what master therapist Dr. Sue Johnson describes as ARE (for accessible, responsive, and emotionally engaged)—qualities we need for a secure bond—that doesn't mean you're destined to be doomed in relationships! It *does* mean that you ended up with an adaptive attachment system, what some therapists will describe as having "insecure attachment." It is possible to shift this, however, in our adult love relationships by building what's called "earned secure attachment." Partners can co-create accessibility, responsiveness, and emotional engagement together and shift the ways enduring vulnerabilities show up. You can actually rewire your nervous systems together!

A Few Words About Language

> Language is very powerful. Language does not just describe reality. Language creates the reality it describes. —DESMOND TUTU, THEOLOGIAN AND HUMAN RIGHTS ACTIVIST

Throughout this book, you'll notice that my choice of language is highly intentional. For example, when it comes to language commonly used to discuss attachment and bonding, the words many researchers and therapists use can end up sounding negative. This is because bonding research initially started with language used to describe babies and little kids. I prefer to use more humanistic strengths-based language to inspire hopefulness, as organized in the chart on page 19.

I also strive to use language that includes and centers marginalized communities—including LGBTQIA+ people and non-heteronormative relationship structures. Though I use the term "partner" for grammatical simplicity, please note that we are including in our discussion relationships that involve more than one partner. My suggestions, tools, and exercises apply to and can be used by relationships with more than two partners.

In addition, trust-recovery work calls for the embrace of "both/and." For example, "I *both* love you more than anyone *and* I'm not sure if I want to stay in a relationship with you." Throughout the book, you'll notice me use "and" in sentences that would sound more natural with "but." The following charts on page 22 show some examples of what I mean by both/and.

Please note, I default to whatever language feels comfortable for clients *and* let them know about some person-centered alternatives preferred by therapists. You'll see the following swaps throughout the book:

"Affair"	"Relational norm violation" or "relationship norm violation" (RNV)
"Cheater"	"Involved partner"
"Cheated"	"Violated relationship norms" or "engaged in a RNV"
"Cheated-on"	"Hurt partner"
"Person they cheated with"	"Affair partner"

Both/And Examples for Hurt Partners

We can . . .	And still . . .
Forgive someone	Not want reconciliation
Empathize	Refuse to condone
Validate	Hold boundaries
Trust again	Always have a "truth meter"
Release detective urges	Feel safe and secure
Have a suspicious part	Be a good, trusting partner
Completely shatter	Feel whole again

Both/And Examples for Involved Partners

We can . . .	And still . . .
Forgive ourselves	Take accountability
Make mistakes	Deserve love and care
Own our choices/actions	Practice self-compassion
Practice self-acceptance	Seek ways to evolve
Connect with guilt and remorse	See ourselves as part of a bigger picture
Really, *reeeally* mess up	Be trusted again and seen as loyal

These word choices not only help reduce shame and increase the chance for positive change, they encompass a wider variety of betrayal experiences. Simply calling a betrayal an "affair" or "infidelity" leaves out increasingly common RNVs like hiding debt or out-of-control behaviors. They also call to mind gender role stereotypes that are often inaccurate and generally unhelpful.

I also like to clarify that we can *both* hold someone accountable and empower them to hold themselves accountable *and* refuse to condone behavior that's clearly unethical and out of alignment with our values. For example, just because I prefer the term "involved partner" over "cheater" does not mean I condone their terrible choices or fail to stand in my power when inviting them to own up to those choices.

I want to be really clear that I'm not in the business of judging or making assumptions. Here are a few things I want you to know about me because it may help to ease your mind:

* Even though I have compassion and empathy for the humanness involved in lying and violating norms, I am distinctly *not* pro-violating relational norms; I hold compassion *and* expect integrity.

* I've done my own therapy to move through betrayal as a hurt partner as well as an involved partner, so my understanding is personal as well as clinical.

* I believe you deserve care and support whether you're casually dating, partnered, cohabitating, or married. I won't judge or blame based on your chosen relationship structure. For example, being more-than-monogamous doesn't make you less deserving of empathy post-RNV.

* I have no agenda beyond illuminating possibilities and providing tools and resources for you.

* I don't judge anyone for either staying in the relationship or for choosing to leave; you're the expert on you.

Finally, you'll see that I don't say "let go" or "get over" when talking about healing in the wake of relational norm violations. Language that reliably helps clients frame what our healthy goals are includes phrases and words such as "move through," "heal through," and "release."

Committed to Healing

> Healing is an art. It takes time. It takes practice. It takes love.
> —PAVANA REDDY, POET BEHIND @MAZADOHTA

If you're a hurt partner impacted by a painful RNV(s), here are a few things to know:

* If you only remember one thing from this book, let it be this: Stabilize *first* and *then* seek insight and understanding. It's normal to want to understand *why* right away, but that's when we are physiologically most flooded and dysregulated, and therefore least able to access areas of the brain needed to approach "why" questions.

* Contempt is the number one relationship killer, according to The Gottman Institute, which has empirically studied the science of relationships for decades. If a critical statement sounds like "I don't like that," a contemptuous statement escalates it to "I don't like that *and* you're a piece of shit because of it." It's normal to feel anger and resentment, and even contempt at times. But beware of bottling emotions and letting anger and disappointment morph into full-on contempt. Releasing it as objective statements of what is troubling you, framed in kind or forgiving language, will be much more palatable and convincing.

* Shame doesn't get people to change—it shuts them down. If you need your partner to change their behavior, invite the part of yourself that tends to want to punish people to take a back seat so that you can focus on making space for you and your partner

to productively process feelings like guilt and remorse. These feelings help us know when our actions are out of alignment with our values.

* Be mindful of trying to control your partner to try to prevent a repeat RNV. If your partner only honors relationship norms because you've given them no choice, that doesn't inspire trust—it just reinforces that we can't trust our partner to make healthy decisions on their own.

If you're an involved partner who violated your relationship's norms, here are a few things to know:

* You can't rush or skip the vulnerable feelings part of this work. If it's hard to allow yourself to do soft emotions, you'll be called to practice being vulnerable so you don't unintentionally dodge or act out against your partner's emotions. If you don't already have an individual therapist or a support group, connecting with one can be incredibly helpful.

* Patience and self-compassion are your best friends. There will be times when the healing process will feel frustrating or unfair because you'll be called on to put pain that was already there *before* the RNV on hold to show up for your hurt partner. I know it's hard *and* I deeply want the hurt partner to eventually be able to hear and understand *your* pain, so we must begin by stabilizing.

* Trauma happens in our bodies when we feel overwhelmed and alone. Remind the problem-solving and solution-focused parts of yourself that being willing to show up and stay with your partner—even in the thick of their sadness, anxiety, panic, and anger—will prevent the toxic aloneness that gets in the way of healing.

Reassurances for Hurt and Involved Partners

Whether you're in the immediate aftermath of a painful relational norm violation or you've soldiered through the hurt for a long time, know that I see you and understand on a very visceral level. There simply aren't sufficient words to capture the full rawness of having been betrayed yet wanting to make an effort to stay with the person who hurt us. Nor are there words to capture the brutal intensity of the daily experience when we've betrayed someone we love and want to rebuild trust.

As we team up to help support you and your relationship, I'd like to offer you the same reassurances I share with clients in my therapy office.

If you're a hurt partner:

* You won't be forced to forgive. If you choose to, you are in charge of the timeline.

* At the beginning of rebuilding trust, the stability and regulation of your nervous system will determine the pace of processing and how deep you go. At any time, if something feels too-much-too-fast, name it.

* While I offer language alternatives and reframes, you have the final say in how to proceed because language creates reality and you're the expert on you. This also applies if it feels like your religious beliefs conflict with my approaches.

* You'll notice me advocate for a slow and steady approach even when you just want to understand everything at once. This isn't an invitation to not ask questions; rather I'm asking for patience so you can ask questions when you're grounded enough to hear and fully understand.

* When I encourage avoiding shame-based language, this is only to give you the best shot at accessing an authentic version of your

partner, not because I'm condoning harmful behaviors like lying or trying to get your partner off the hook.

* At some point in the process, we will look at the big picture to see how y'all got set up for the betrayal experience(s) and ways your role in the relationship's dynamic could have possibly contributed. But rest assured, you will never be blamed for your partner's RNV(s).

* If RNVs keep repeating, even when partners have done individual therapy and you've done relational work together, it can be worth considering whether the structure of the relationship or the relationship itself is really right for everyone.

If you're an involved partner:

* You won't be asked to self-flagellate, take full responsibility for every hurtful thing ever committed, or pointlessly rehash painful events and moments forever.

* During the immediate aftermath of the RNV and the early stage of rebuilding trust, you will notice a focus on stabilizing the hurt partner that can feel unfair. Know that I'm fully aware you might have been holding the bulk of the hurt in a relationship when the RNV occurred, and it can be hard to hear we won't be able to deeply address your pre-RNV emotional reality until your partner stabilizes. Your partner needs to be able to hear and understand you, so an initial focus on their stabilization benefits everyone.

* Your pain is valid. Just because you violated norms in your relationship doesn't mean you give up your right to have and demonstrate feelings. That said, at first you'll have to look to an outside source—like an individual therapist and/or confidential best friend—for emotional support because it isn't a right use of

power to ask that hurt partners meet your needs when they aren't yet stable enough to regulate themselves.

* There will be times you'll feel your patience tested and integrity questioned—even if you're no longer violating norms. Continuing to show up is what's going to help. I get how frustrating and heartbreaking it can feel when our words have lost their ability to soothe and reassure our partner. You'll be able to feel that superpower again—but it will take dedication, consistency and time.

* If RNVs keep repeating, even when partners have done individual therapy and you've done relational work together, it can be worth considering whether the structure of the relationship is really right for everyone. Regarding opening up relationships: If you're truly in love with an affair partner, the possibility of connecting with this person may not be off the table. However, *how* you engage during trust-recovery work can ruin any shot at keeping that possibility on the table. If this person loves and respects you, they'll understand the temporary need for a wide berth and things like increased transparency around communication in the meantime.

A final note for all partners: If it's been more than six to eight weeks since the disclosure/discovery of an RNV and you do not feel able to discuss the RNV without a blowup, you're feeling so distressed that it's significantly disrupting your daily life, and/or you are experiencing symptoms related to trauma (e.g., hypervigilance, panic attacks, insomnia and/or nightmares, severe anxiety, social isolation, etc.), then you may need to seek professional support.

How to Use This Book

Trust that if y'all were sitting with me, Morgan, in my office, you'd see a warm smile looking back at you, and a playful lady who is ready to help you look for new possibilities, doorways to self-compassion, and trailheads that mark areas for adventurous exploration and healing. I hope that same feeling comes across in these pages.

There are multiple ways to utilize this book, including:

* In conjunction with relationship counseling/therapy (be sure to let your therapist know!).

* As an individual interested in learning about rebuilding trust.

* On a schedule that's agreeable to everyone. For example, "We'll read one chapter every two to three weeks and schedule time to discuss and try any tools appropriate for us."

* In a clinical setting as a helping professional working with clients.

* To organize a supportive book group (for instance, in a pastoral counseling setting or women's group).

The book is organized into two parts. In Part I, I support you as you begin stabilizing and navigating the complex process of healing after betrayals of trust. Part II will inspire partners who want to further strengthen their relationship. Within each chapter, you'll find tools such as journaling prompts, conversation starters and templates, skill-building activities, and therapy-based strategies. If your relationship is still freshly in the aftermath of someone disclosing or discovering betrayal, or it's been a while but you never really processed it together, I invite you to start with Part I, Chapter 1. Otherwise, feel free to skip around and read chapters that seem most relevant in this moment and pick and choose tools that feel like they best address your current needs.

As you'll see, most of the tools in this book require access to a quiet, calm area with few interruptions. This is not the kind of book you'd want to bust out in the airport to work on together! If there are any materials required, I'll note them at the beginning of each tool. I also include a list of "Prep Questions" for each tool. These are things to consider individually or journal about before partners meet to try a particular tool. At the end of the book on page 186, I share a list of "feelings" words that can help you describe your internal experiences in a neutral way, without implying anything about your partner's actions or intentions.

Let's get started.

Part 1
STABILIZE AND REPAIR

WHEN WE'RE REELING in the wake of a disclosure or discovery of a betrayal, the last thing we want to hear is a therapist saying how important it is to *slow down*. The emotional devastation is so blistering for everyone involved that we want relief *yesterday*. I totally get that, and I'd like to share what sex researcher and educator Emily Nagoski says in her book *Come As You Are*. She describes emotions as tunnels: "You have to go all the way through the darkness to get to the light." If you grew up in an emotion-dismissing environment, allowing yourself to feel vulnerable emotions can feel scary. Remind yourself that it's not the darkness that's dangerous—it's getting stuck in it and losing sight of the light at the end.

Most of the evidence-based clinical models favored by contemporary trust-recovery therapists involve three stages that include the following main tasks:

1. Deescalating, stabilizing, and atonement
2. Shifting/restructuring unhealthy patterns and increasing attunement as well as insight and understanding
3. Integrating new skills to tackle past and future problems together, and co-creating secure attachment and a vision for the future together

To that end, in the first part of our work together, we'll focus on strategies for slowing down, stabilizing, and creating a felt sense of emotional safety together. When I say *safety,* I mean specifically in the nervous system sense—do our attachment systems have a felt sense of safety? Can we feel grounded and alert without feeling agitated or numb? Does our partner consistently show up as what relationship therapist and author Sue Johnson calls ARE: accessible when we need them, responsive when we reach out, and emotionally engaged? That's what "safe" really means to our bodies and brains.

You'll walk away with greater appreciation for the importance of checking in before using a tool or trying to process something together and recognizing when breaks are needed and taking them. I know it can be tempting to rush ahead to tasks like seeking insight and understanding, but if we don't allow ourselves adequate space and time to get grounded, we won't be able to access the part of our brain that allows us to think into the future and make judgments and decisions.

Morgan's General Emergency Trust First Aid Recommendations

While there's no one-size-fits-all approach to rebuilding trust, over the years I've seen a number of common pitfalls that clients can experience as they grapple with their loss and altered sense of relationship reality. Often they are overwhelmed and off-balance, especially if it's only been days to weeks from the disclosure or discovery of the RNV. These recommendations can save you a lot of grief as you begin to process a betrayal.

* Take your time. The vast majority of couples who work with me end up choosing to stay together. You'll have time to make those decisions. For today, just decide how you'll care for yourself and offer care if you've negatively impacted a partner. Remember: Slow and stabilize *first, then* try for insight and understanding when your brain is fully online again.

* No one gets to tell anyone if or when they should forgive or reconcile. If you're reacting from a fear-based place, resolve to wait to make decisions. Regrets are more likely to happen if things move quickly and automatically rather than slowly and intentionally.

* Agree together who to tell—and when and how. Limit disclosures to as few people as possible. This isn't hiding in response to feelings of shame, but rather deciding to take back power together by being mindful about if and how to share.

* Cease contact with affair partner(s) for the time being and consider ways to avoid future contact. (This goes for involved partners *and* hurt partners!) If you need to continue contact (because you work with the affair partner or they're in the family), agree together on how to make this feel as transparent and safe as possible.

* Consider hiring a professional with trust-recovery experience to guide you through the process. That investment can turn a process that might take *years* on your own into a matter of weeks to a few months—it can be worth it!

* If you're a hurt partner, keep a running list of questions you want to ask when the time is right. A relationship or individual counselor can help you think about timing, as can the information you'll learn in this book. Another option: download Esther Perel's free "Infidelity Resource Guide" for guidance.

* During conversations with your partner, use "name it to tame it" (see page 104). Don't just say "I understand" but identify your partner's feelings and repeat your partner's exact words back to them (for example, "You feel hurt and betrayed. I lied."). Naming feelings this way calms our amygdala—a threat-detecting part of our brain that can trigger survival mode responses such as fight-or-flight or freeze.

* Patience and self-compassion are your best friends. If you lied, you may have lost your voice for a while. Release urges to explain, convince, and justify—focus on showing up with actions. If you were lied to, focus on slowing down and healing. Trust that showing yourself compassion will allow for understanding once you're grounded enough to process more deeply.

CHAPTER ONE

Reestablish Safety

When the present falls apart,
so does the future we had associated
with it. And having the future taken
away is the mother of all plot twists.

—LORI GOTTLIEB, THERAPIST AND AUTHOR

THE NECESSARY FOUNDATION for all of the hard work we will do together is a feeling of safety for all partners. In this chapter, our goal will be to work together to rebuild—or to build for the first time—a safe space. We will begin to learn to support each other's vulnerabilities and increase stability, predictability, and transparency. We will work on helping to soothe and reassure one another when one or more partners is feeling distressed or dysregulated, or when a conflict cycle happens. Learning to self-soothe and to invite your partner to do the same will become important tools as well. The increased accessibility, responsiveness, and emotional engagement we come away from this chapter with will set the stage for progress as we continue on through the book.

It's incredibly important to establish safety before starting emotion-triggering discussions together. Establishing safety goes hand in hand with our partner's consistency in showing us that they're accessible, responsive, and emotionally engaged.

Another way of thinking about emotional safety is the Gottman ATTUNE acronym, which helps us define "attunement" and recognize the skills needed to build trust:

A **Awareness** of our and our partner's internal worlds

T **Turning Toward** each other by noticing when our partner reaches for us, and responding in ways they can feel

T **Tolerance** of distress, dissonance, differing perspectives, dialectics, etc.

U **Understanding** of our and our partner's feelings, needs, wants, longings, and fears

N **Non-Defensive Responding** by actively listening without defending/blaming/attacking

E **Empathy,** which is feeling what someone is feeling *with* them

Building a Safe Relationship Space

FOR: PARTNERS TOGETHER

What You'll Learn

* How to co-create a safe space where everyone feels supported.

* How to intentionally bond together to shift negative beliefs that were created early in life or post-RNV. For example, "It's not safe for me to trust you" or "You won't be there when I need you most."

What You'll Need

* 1 to 1.5 hours (plus at least 30 minutes for prep/journaling)

* Paper or digital notepad for listing co-agreements

THIS TOOL WILL help you agree on guidelines for discussions. As you work through the steps below, you'll create a list of guidelines specific to your relationship. Some helpful suggestions from Stan Tatkin of the PACT Institute:

1. Agree on a single topic and set a time limit.
2. Talk slowly and make eye contact.
3. Rapidly relieve pain by naming any big, vulnerable feelings.
4. Aim to be "Okay for now."

Goals

Practice talking about the relationship without escalating into conflict or disconnection.

Understand what each person needs to feel safe enough to share and be vulnerable.

Prep Questions

* What helps me feel safe in my body during conflict? What if I freeze? What if I get anxious?

* When I feel emotionally unsettled and reactive, what does my partner do and say that feels soothing, reassuring, or nurturing?

* How do I know when I need a time-out? What sensations do I specifically notice in my body (my heart starts racing and my palms feel clammy)? Am I able to communicate that when it happens? If not, can I give a physical signal requesting a time-out?

Instructions

1. Prepare your Safe Relationship Space.
   * Set a timer and agree that the goal is to list conversation co-agreements—guidelines everyone will respect when trying to communicate. If you're experiencing a lot of conflict, begin with just 20 minutes and build up to longer conversations. It's better to have a few short, neutral-to-positive experiences than to keep derailing while trying for something longer.
   * If you do not complete the entire list, just be sure to agree on a time to circle back and continue working on the agreements.

2. Think through these questions together:
   * How will we schedule time for our conversations?
   * What rituals will we engage in to mark that we are opening our Safe Relationship Space? (For example, some couples I work with sit at the kitchen table together and light a candle to differentiate this time from a regular chat.)
   * If one of us gets triggered, how will we close the conversation space and switch gears into an emotional support role?
   * If everyone becomes flooded at the same time, how will we take a time-out?
   * If we take a time-out, how will make sure that we don't sweep things under the rug? How will we schedule a time to try again?

SAMPLE CONVERSATION CO-AGREEMENTS LIST

* When one of us needs to talk about something, we say *specifically* what we want to process. For example, "Can we use our Safe

Relationship Space to process how I'm feeling about the affair partner this week?"

* We sit down together on the couch where we can be face-to-face and set a timer.

* We take care of our individual bodies as we begin by being aware of our breathing.

* We work together to stay slow and soft and redirect ourselves if we start blaming or becoming defensive.

* We keep things confidential and agree on whom we share intimate details with outside the relationship.

* We notice if we are trying to problem-solve when we need to just be reflecting and validating each other so we can shift gears back to emotional support, not "fixing."

* We describe *our* feelings, needs, and fears, *not* our partner's, and we avoid sarcasm.

* We share with "I messages," as in "I feel _____ (name feeling) when I hear you say _____," and don't start sentences with "You always/never . . ." or "Well, you . . ."

* We aim to avoid each other's triggers *and* simply validate and support if we bump into one.

* If one of us feels overwhelmed, we make the time-out signal with our hands, which means we stop trying to verbally process for 20 minutes, then try again with more softness after any needed apologies are made.

* We don't use our agreements as weapons to threaten or police each other—they are just helpful guidelines to keep us on track.

Seven Ways to Complete the Stress-Response Cycle

FOR: INDIVIDUALS AND PARTNERS, SEPARATELY

IMAGINE THAT EVERY time you gear up to deal with stress, your body pumps out stress hormones like water being poured into a glass. If you don't use these hormones—for instance, if you have to listen to your boss yell at you without running away or punching them in the face—the hormones stay in your body, collecting in that glass. This is called an "incomplete stress-response cycle."

Now imagine that glass of water at the end of the day. It might be overflowing! If we don't do something to empty the glass, we're more likely to experience symptoms like anxiety and depression. These strategies will help you empty that glass.

What You'll Learn

* How to be more grounded and regulated for emotional conversations and processing together.

* Actions that can complete the stress-response cycle when you're activated.

What You'll Need

* 30 minutes to 1 hour

Goals

Identify things each person in the relationship can do individually to complete stress-response cycles.

Identify activities partners can do together and/or with the family to complete stress-response cycles.

Prep Questions

* When do I feel most relaxed each day? When do I generally feel most relaxed throughout the month?

* Are there certain times of year (for instance, hot summer or cold winter) when I'm more limited in my ability to comfortably move through the world?

* What stressors are present that I can't avoid? (coping with the RNV) Which ones can I step away and get a break from? (stressful boss at work)

Instructions

1. Look over this list of evidence-based ways to complete the stress-response cycle:
   * Physical activity
   * Mindful breathing
   * Positive social interaction
   * Laughter
   * Affection (with a partner, friend, family member, and/or pet)
   * Having a "big ol' cry"
   * Creative expression

2. Use these items to create one individual SMART goal for completing stress-response cycles in your body and one SMART goal you can have as a team. The acronym "SMART" refers to goals that are Specific, Measurable, Attainable, Realistic, and Timely.

   For example, "Every Monday, Wednesday, and Friday, we'll walk the dogs together for at least thirty minutes after breakfast before we start our workday routines. Each month, during our relationship check-in, we'll think about how we did with the goals and make any changes as needed."

   On _____ days each week, I commit to _____.

   On _____ days each week, we commit to _____.

Process or Pause?

FOR: PARTNERS TOGETHER

"Put your oxygen mask on before assisting others."
"We can't pour from an empty cup."

The goal of this tool is to help you recognize when your brain needs a break. Our brains take a lot of energy to run, especially the cerebral cortex, which enables *executive function*, which includes judgment, decision-making, planning, and thinking about the future. This is why the old adage "Don't go to bed angry" is so hated by therapists working from the interpersonal neurobiology framework! We know it's common to want to have conversations at the end of the day when there's some downtime *and* that's also when you're likely most tired and at highest risk of miscommunication. So, *do* go to bed angry and agree to process together in the daylight, when your brains are well-rested and functioning at their optimal levels.

If you know someone who has ever done recovery work for substance use, you might be familiar with the acronym HALT, which reminds people to pause and check if they are feeling Hungry, Angry, Lonely, Tired—states that can make people more susceptible to self-destructive behaviors. The invitation here is similar. If you're feeling any of these things, address them before having important conversations with your partner.

If one or more people would like to open the Safe Relationship Space for conversation but there's awareness that someone is triggered/reactive/dysregulated/activated, whoever has the awareness is invited to ask, "Process or pause?"

What You'll Learn

* How to assess whether you're regulated and emotionally available enough to show up to your Safe Relationship Space.

* How to check in with each other to decide together if you're able to communicate vulnerably and be attuned to each other.

What You'll Need

* At least 20 minutes

> ### Goals
>
> Be able to identify readiness for conversation individually and together.
>
> Practice pausing and meeting individual needs *before* opening your Safe Relationship Space.

Prep Questions

* How can I tell when I'm not emotionally available for a Safe Relationship Space conversation? What sensations or feelings do I notice in my body when I am *not* ready to talk?

* Growing up, was I ever forced to have conversations when I wasn't ready?

Instructions

1. Go through the following checklist of "readiness questions" individually, prior to having a serious conversation relating to your healing process or anything having to do with the recovery of relationship trust. Ask yourself, am I feeling:

    * Rested? (Have I gotten enough sleep? Do I need a nap or a full night's rest first?)
    * Nourished? (Have I had enough food and water? Do I need a snack or water first?)
    * Grounded? (Do I feel relatively calm? Do I need to take a walk first?)
    * Resourced? (Do I have what I need to feel self-compassionate and confident? Do I have the emotional bandwidth? Do I need to talk to my therapist or close friend first?)

2. Let each other know how you're feeling in each of these areas. Some couples like to use "Red-Yellow-Green" as shorthand to let each other know the status of their nervous systems. "Green" means that you're able to engage—you feel emotionally safe and grounded. "Yellow" means that you're on the verge of being dysregulated, but you could try processing and see if there's enough safety to get into green. "Red" means you're not available to emotionally connect right now but will try again later.

3. If you agree you're ready to process, continue reading for processing tools! If you need to pause and are worried that things might not be circled back to, ask your partner to help reassure you that it won't be forgotten, and don't forget to agree on a time to revisit.

Reminder: Things don't have to be *perfect* in order to process, *and* if you answer a strong "no" to any of the readiness questions in the Instructions above, address those needs first and only then agree to return to processing.

Taking Breaks and Time-Outs

FOR: PARTNERS TOGETHER

What You'll Learn

* How to ask for a break when you need one and how to ask if your partner needs a break without blaming or escalating.

* How to co-create a comfortable break-taking ritual.

What You'll Need

* At least 20 minutes

DEPENDING ON THE way our attachment system gets wired in early life, some of us prefer to do emotional processing out loud with other people (interpersonal processors), and some of us need some solitude before reporting back to partners (internal processors). It's also normal if you do both!

It gets a little tricky when partners' processing styles are different and one person tends to withdraw while another longs to immediately process together. When that happens, one partner's need for a break needs to be balanced with another partner's worries that taking a break means never tackling the topic. I recommend taking a half-hour break and then trying to reengage since it can take the nervous system at least twenty minutes to return to baseline when someone is dysregulated.

Goals

Practice taking time to soothe and down-regulate your body without ruminating on why you're upset with your partner or listing a rap sheet for them.

Increase patience and a healthy tolerance for discomfort.

Prep Questions

* If I tend to need space and my partner does not, what stories or explanations do I tell myself about this?

✳ If my partner needs space/time to internally process and it's trigger-ing for me to wait, in what healthy ways can I distract myself or take care of myself during that time?

Instructions

Read over the following prompts individually and complete them together:

We each know we need to take a break when we can sense _____.

Signs (physical, emotional, relational) that my partner is getting dysregu-lated include: _____.

If one of us is unaware that we've flooded, we can check in with each other by asking, "_____?" ("Is that flooding thing happening for you?" Be specific about what language feels best; if someone tends to get defensive, "Are you flooding?" can cue a default "No, I'm not!" defensive response.)

If asking about our emotions triggers one or more of us, we will use a physical gesture or touch to check in, specifically _____ (a light-touch hand on the shoulder or seeking eye contact) that we'll know means, "Should we slow or time-out?"

We will initiate the time-out together by setting a timer for at least 20 minutes, then we will check back in with each other to see if we're regulated enough by _____ (sitting eye-to-eye in our special spot).

Our ritual for cushioning one another with positivity and appreciation when we are coming back together after taking a time-out specifies that we will _____ (hug until we feel relaxed together then sit down to try to talk again; each list something we appreciate about the other person; hold hands and make eye contact while saying "same team").

Negative to Neutral, Neutral to Positive

FOR: PARTNERS TOGETHER

What You'll Learn

* How to frame healthy expectations around trust recovery.

* How to use neutral-to-positive experiences to provide cushioning (insulate with positive interactions to counter criticisms) so normal relational conflict doesn't continue to erode trust.

What You'll Need

* About 6 hours per week, but don't worry if that feels impossible. If the relationship is distressed, any increase in intentional time is beneficial.

IN TRUST-RECOVERY COUNSELING, we have to be clear on what to expect because the work is hard and we need to recognize and celebrate the "little things" we achieve together. We cannot expect an overnight turnaround—in fact, it can be unwise to trust anything that looks like a sudden, miraculous 180-degree change. When there's been RNV(s), we must shift from negative to neutral before we can go from neutral to positive.

After an RNV, it's normal for partners to spend hours together analyzing the relationship. It's important to also share some intentional neutral-to-positive time in order to provide enough cushioning for the difficult emotional processing work. This can be something as simple as sitting together and watching a show on Netflix that you both like. I tell clients that anything non-harmful that feels "distinctly not-awful" counts at the start.

Goals

Spend time together that's distinctly not-awful to retrain your nervous systems to see partners as safe allies.

Practice slowing, stabilizing, and finding footing *before* preparing to try to understand.

Practice embodying patience while managing parts of yourselves that might want to rush to fix or problem-solve.

Tip: If you have a strong fixer/problem-solver part of you, tell those parts that trying to fix or problem-solve too soon *is* the problem. Understand, or at least entertain, the idea that emotional presence and attunement are needed first to bring back trust.

Prep Questions

✳ When do I feel most neutral (or least awful) around my partner? When do/did I feel most positively toward them? When do I feel most neutral-to-positive as an individual lately?

✳ Do I need some individual support or space to process any feelings of frustration and/or disappointment around framing a key goal as getting to neutral? (Internally, this frustration might sound like, "Great, so the best I can hope for right now is just not-awful? How are we ever going to get to feeling *good*?")

Instructions

1. Individually, generate a list of two or three things you can do by yourself that feel neutral-to-positive and share these with your partner.

2. Together, list five things you can do with each other that feel neutral-to-positive. This can include "parallel play," where you're doing separate things nearby. (For example, "I work on my painting while you do some woodworking" or "You play a video game while I read my book.")

3. Agree on when and where you'll hang out together and put this on your calendars.

4. Check in with each other weekly to consider whether you got in some neutral-to-positive time together more days than not. If not, what is getting in the way and how can you team up to address it?

5. Let your partner know something you appreciate about how they're showing up in the trust-recovery process. ("Thanks for continuing to show up, even when it's really hard"; "I appreciate you re-committing to honesty"; "It means a lot to me that you're willing to give me a chance to change and atone.")

6. Complete these sentences:
   a. Things I can do to feel more open and neutral-to-positive individually include: _____, _____, _____.
   b. Things we can do with each other that feel distinctly not-awful or even positive include: _____, _____, _____, _____, _____.

Creating Safe Spaces with Active Listening

FOR: PARTNERS TOGETHER AND/OR WITH FAMILY AND FRIENDS

WHEN THERE'S BEEN an RNV, it can be an uncomfortable wake-up call that we have stopped listening to one another. When a relationship isn't flourishing, partners are often doing a lot of talking and *feel* like they're listening, but they've actually just gotten into a pattern of monologuing at each other, waiting for their turn to make their point instead of truly and deeply hearing and understanding.

Therapists are trained to support partners to learn to listen to each other. While it can definitely be easier to disrupt communication patterns with a therapist there to help stop you, considering the guidelines therapists learn can help us begin to steer ourselves in healthier directions.

I like to keep these words from relationship specialist Dr. John Gottman in mind: "Remember that behind every negative emotion there is a longing, and a wish, and therefore a recipe for your partner to be successful with you. That is your positive need. What do you want and need from your partner?"

What You'll Learn

* Ways to improve at listening and hearing the heart of things.

* How to share in ways that make it easier for partners to listen and respond non-defensively. (It's not our job to keep partners from getting defensive, but we have the ability to help them.)

What You'll Need

* At least 20 minutes

Goals

Redirect parts of yourself that want to convince or change someone and challenge yourself to tune in to what those parts want, need, or long for.

Practice distilling emotional experiences down to a clear message—a specific feeling, need, fear, longing—without speaking for so long that your partner gets lost or begins to feel defensive.

Practice being with someone without trying to problem-solve or move into solution-focused mode. The goal isn't a quick fix, to avoid all conflict, but to soothe and reassure ourselves and each other when conflict cycles inevitably happen.

Prep Questions

* Was it easy for me to feel seen and heard when growing up? Who listened to me when I was upset? What were their responses and pieces of advice?

* Growing up, what did I learn about talking about feelings? If it's uncomfortable to feel feelings, what self-compassion can I offer myself to appreciate why it's hard for me? ("It's challenging for me to talk about feelings when I never saw anyone do it and was called a sissy if I ever showed soft emotions.")

* What does my partner do and say that helps me to feel seen, heard, and understood? (If you can't think of anything easily, what does a close friend or family member do that helps?)

* When do I feel most unseen and misunderstood? What helps me when that happens?

Instructions

Take turns being Speaker and Listener. If one person tends to withdraw when feeling emotionally vulnerable or dysregulated, invite this partner to be Speaker first. Agree to use this tool as a helpful resource, not a way to call each other out for being imperfect as we practice this together.

SPEAKER

* State needs in a positive way. ("I need you to talk with me about x this evening" instead of "I don't want you to keep avoiding discussing this with me.")

* Start sentences with "I," stating a current need. Avoid blaming. ("I felt devastated when I heard you lie to me.")

* Make sure you're sharing feelings, not thoughts/beliefs. ("I feel like you should have done x" is an opinion, not a feeling.)

* Use "I" statements about specific situations, not vague generalizations. ("I felt disappointed when I came home and the dishes had not been finished when you promised to do them" instead of "I feel let down by you all the time.")

Remember that this type of listening might be a new skill for your partner. Give them some grace and ask yourself, "Is my partner showing up authentically, bravely, and vulnerably even if it's super hard for them?" If you aren't sure what you need right now, it's fair to name something like, "I'm still trying to understand what I need. Right now, I do know I need spaces like the one we are trying to co-create here to name things out loud and feel your presence and validation."

LISTENER

* Set aside your agenda so you can hear *and* repeat the Speaker's perspective back to them. Try to listen compassionately for what is hurting your partner. Hear your partner's feelings and allow yourself to feel some of them.

* Listener will first repeat back content to check for understanding. Be specific with language and use the exact emotion words you hear your partner use. For example, instead of simply saying, "I under- stand," say, "I hear that you're feeling betrayed and totally lost."

* Next, validate by saying something like, "It makes sense to me that you'd feel that way and have these needs because _____."

* Try asking: "Is there more? What does it feel like I'm still not getting?"

HOW DID WE DO?

* Share with each other one thing you appreciated about their listening/validating/sharing.

* Share one thing that felt difficult that you'd like to work on as an individual. ("I want to be able to self-soothe better in the moment to stay more present emotionally.")

* Name one request for your partner to consider next time. ("I felt really cared for when you were owning your impact. In the future, will you be extra mindful of how I can get triggered when you describe what you assume my feelings are instead of asking me?")

Embodying Trustworthiness

FOR: INVOLVED PARTNERS, INDIVIDUALLY

WHEN WE'VE ENGAGED in an RNV and/or lying and gas-lighting, one of the most common, heart-wrenching experiences is noticing that our former ability—superpower even—to soothe and reassure our partner disappears for a while. Whatever we used to say or do that helped suddenly falls flat, gets ignored, or inspires an adverse reaction.

It's normal for hurt partners to report that one part of them wants one thing, while at the exact same time, another part wants something completely opposite. A hurt partner may want their partners to hold, kiss, and soothe them in their pain—at the same time, it doesn't feel safe anymore. This "come close to me but get away from me!" roller coaster can last for a few weeks to months, depending on the nature of the RNV(s).

If you're a problem-solver, the first stage of recovery work, in which you're de-escalating and stabilizing the relationship, can feel especially challenging because it calls for a lot of stillness, repetition, and tasks that don't necessarily *seem* like solutions. My TRUSTED acronym on the next page can help give fix-it parts of yourself something to focus on while you're waiting patiently for the hurt partner and the relationship to stabilize enough to move to the next stage of rebuilding trust.

What You'll Learn

* Seven things to focus on that actively *show* your partner that you're someone they can trust.

* How to track when it's safe to invite others to put their trust in us.

What You'll Need

* 1 hour or more

* Paper and pen or digital notepad for journaling

> ### Goals
>
> Decrease frustration and felt sense of helplessness by focusing on what you *can* do.
>
> Help reassure parts of you that are concerned about "doing the right thing."
>
> Focus on actions and behaviors that embody your apology, not just saying the words.

Prep Questions

✳ How does it feel to reframe my goals in this healing process? What's coming up for me?

✳ What kinds of support systems do I need to support me for account-ability, healing, and growth? Do I need to schedule a session with my individual therapist or find one?

Instructions

Consider the following questions based on TRUSTED and allow yourself to reflect and/or journal. Feel invited to share with your partner what this experience was like for you!

CAN I BE TRUSTED? PROMPTS

TAKE CARE OF BUSINESS

How will I show that I'm committed to changing with actions that align with my words and values? What concrete actions can I do? (Find a ther-apist and begin self-exploration, go to a support group, etc.) Remember to *show, don't tell*. Especially if you engaged in lying or gaslighting and you've temporarily "lost your voice." Action is the currency your partner will accept until there's been enough time to repeatedly show that you can safely trust yourself and ask others to trust you.

MAKE TIMELY **R**EPAIRS

How can I be a good steward of this relationship and support us to make well-timed repairs when one or more of us is feeling hurt? If I catch myself doing something that negatively impacts my partner, can I shorten the time between the impact of my behavior and my partner hearing my apology?

INCREASE **U**NDERSTANDING OF PARTNER'S INTERNAL WORLD(S)

How can I ask questions to increase my understanding of my partner's internal world(s)? What might I not know about my partner? If I'm having a hard time feeling curious about them, what parts of me might be getting between me and my curiosity?

SLOW AND SOFTEN

How will I show my partner that there's no rush or timeline for healing? If I do feel in a hurry or notice myself pushing for forgiveness on my timeline, how can I own that and reassure my partner that forgiveness is not expected, much less owed? What do I need to support my patience in focusing on stabilizing during this stage of trust recovery? If I'm feeling resentment or contempt, where is there some softness for my partner and what they're going through? How can I tell they're working hard for us too?

TURN TOWARD BIDS FOR CONNECTION

How can I get better at noticing when my partner wants to connect emotionally? Do I know how to recognize when they are making *bids* (requests) for me to *turn toward* them and respond with accessibility and emotional engagement that matches the request?

INCREASE **E**MPATHY AND MAKE ROOM FOR REMORSE

How will I keep myself from burning out while continuing to allow myself to to feel empathy—to let myself feel the hard things my partner is feeling? Do I feel able to imagine how it feels being my partner? Are there any parts of me standing between me and my empathic part? What do I need to be able to let myself feel?

DECREASE **D**EFENSIVENESS

What do I feel when I start getting defensive? What's the story I tell myself about me? What's the story I tell myself about my partner? How can I notice more readily when my defensiveness is kicking in and rein it in, narrating my story objectively? What triggers are the hottest buttons for me still? How am I working on reducing their charge?

Reassurance Recipes

FOR: PARTNERS TOGETHER

WHEN WE AGREE to build a long-term, committed partnership, we don't become 100 percent responsible for our partner's feelings, *and* we take on an increased level of responsibility when we make the choice to bond and co-regulate with someone. In other words, we are taking on a certain level of responsibility for helping our partner regulate their nervous system. We are not *entirely* responsible for the state of their nervous system, *and* because we've committed, we have a special power to help partners get grounded.

Intersectionality is a term coined by Kimberlé Crenshaw to highlight how factors like race, gender, socioeconomic status, and other traits overlap and intersect, making our experiences unique. Cedar Barstow, author of *Right Use of Power*, highlights the importance of acknowledging intersectionality and our individual privileges and power differences when taking accountability for our impact on others and making things right.

Following the work of Crenshaw, Barstow, and Jean Baker Miller, my colleague Gena St. David, who is a therapist, professor, and author, suggests that we embody justice when we work to ensure that compassion flows first to anyone with less power and privilege *before* ourselves. She states that the right use of power is to actively center those who experience the most marginalization and oppression. For example, if we have more power than someone else, it's like we're standing higher up on a hill and they're standing below—compassion

What You'll Learn

* What your partner is able to deeply absorb in terms of reassurance.
* How to ask your partner for reassurance when you're feeling vulnerable.

What You'll Need

* 30 minutes or more

must flow first *downhill* toward the person with least privilege/power if we are being ethical, good stewards of the relationship. If someone with less power/privilege pushes compassion *uphill* toward the one with more power/privilege first, that's grace—but it shouldn't be forced or expected.

What does this mean in the context of rebuilding trust within a relationship? When we lie, we take away some power from our partner. They are then forced to make decisions without the full data set that we're privileged to—they lose some free will. Ethically then, it follows that we now have an increased responsibility to prioritize them as receivers of compassion—even though we are also experiencing suffering and difficulty.

What I'm getting at is this: it's restorative and corrective for you to pour compassion into your hurt partner *without* expecting a matched effort at first. Trust that once your hurt partner has stabilized and the relationship is feeling more secure, there *will* be time and space for insight and a deeper level of understanding into *your* pain and what set the relationship up for the RNV. Involved partners, make sure you have a therapist or trusted friend who *does* have capacity to focus on pouring compassion into you.

Some of us have grown up in an environment where we never really felt reassured or comfortable asking for help. If that's the case for you, it's okay if you aren't sure what helps you feel emotionally cared for. Just keep your radar hot and let your partner know if or when they do something that hits the spot!

Hurt partners, it's normal and okay to say something along the lines of, "I see you offering reassurance in the ways I've voiced needing. I can't fully take it in right now with where we are in the rebuilding trust process, *and* I really appreciate you."

Goals

Be able to express what you need from your partner on an individual level to sense/feel reassured.

Enhance ability to co-regulate when one or more partners are feeling distressed/dysregulated.

✶ Growing up, what did I learn to do if I was sad, upset, or confused? What did I learn about going to others for emotional support, reassurance, or TLC? How did I learn that?

✶ What have my partners/closest friends(s)upports done during tough times in the past that made me feel the most reassured? What have people tried that doesn't really help me?

Instructions

Using the Reassurance Recipes below, take turns sharing with each other what you need to feel soothed and reassured.

REASSURANCE RECIPES

When I'm distressed but not fully flooded, you can help soothe and reassure me by _____ (*making eye contact and saying, "I love you and I'm not going anywhere;" asking if I need to take a break, etc.*).

When I'm flooded and/or unable to take in reassurance from you, I really just need _____ (*30 minutes by myself to cool off; a hug and kiss; to hear "I love you, and we'll figure it out," etc.*).

In certain contexts, for example when _____, I really just need verbal reassurance. That might sound like, _____. In other contexts, like _____, I'm more in need of _____.

In the past, I have felt most reassured by you when you _____ (*specific action*), like the time you _____ (*specific example[s]*). What I really loved about what you did and how it felt was _____.

In addition to being open to accepting your support and reassurance, I can self-soothe when I'm feeling distressed by _____.

CHAPTER TWO

Cultivate Self-Awareness

> The attempt to escape from pain
> is what creates more pain.
>
> —GABOR MATÉ, PHYSICIAN AND AUTHOR

IN THIS CHAPTER, we're going to work on the ability to notice shifts and changes in your autonomic nervous system and learn to support yourself individually and to reach for support from your partner when needed. We'll look at how your moves during the "conflict dance" connect to your attachment wiring and answer questions such as, "How can my partner and I team up to use our relationship to show younger parts of ourselves that things are safe and can be different now?" We'll increase tolerance for discomfort when feeling and sharing about vulnerable emotions and prepare to lay the foundation for eventually moving into insight and understanding.

Wounded Healers

We're all the products of imperfect, flawed caregivers. As adults, we can hold *both* the fact that our parents or caregivers did the best they could *and* the understanding that we needed something more, less, or different. The better we understand the wounds we carry, the less likely we are to be thrown off-balance when those wounds get rubbed the wrong way in relationships.

To become aware of ways you experienced wounding while growing up, I invite you to color in any segment of the chart that feels true for you.

Share with your partner how it feels looking at your chart. What vulnerable feelings show up? What protective parts of you get stirred up when thinking about your partner's unmet needs growing up? It's helpful to recognize the ways in which we and our partners were wounded early in life because it impacts our default coping responses. We want to understand these early experiences and wounds not because we condone unwanted or unpleasant behavior as adults, but because it helps us make sense of our partners, which can make space for more empathy and compassion.

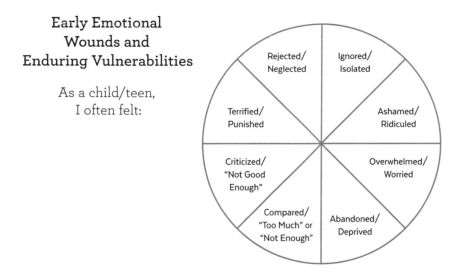

Early Emotional Wounds and Enduring Vulnerabilities

As a child/teen, I often felt:

Our Enduring Vulnerabilities

FOR: PARTNERS TOGETHER AND INDIVIDUALLY

What You'll Learn

* To begin noticing if an emotional-relational trigger roots back to 1) attachment injuries from the current relationship, 2) attachment injuries from all previous love relationships, and/or 3) early attachment wounds from caregiver(s).

What You'll Need

* 1 hour or more

* Paper and pen or digital notepad for journaling

IF WE HAVEN'T spent much time reflecting or working with a counselor to understand ourselves, it can feel confusing—like a rug being pulled out from under us—when we get drawn into a conflict cycle with our partner. The good news is that we don't need to have done a decade of individual therapy to show up in the ways our partners need. What *does* help is having a map. With this tool, you'll begin to create that map and be able to use it to help your partner empathize more deeply. While we can't *make* someone more emotionally responsive to us, we can make ourselves a safe place for them to land. If we increase our self-awareness and ability to contextualize our responses and default coping strategies—points on the map for our partners—it makes it easier for them to hear and respond to us when stressed. As Harriet Lerner says in *The Dance of Anger,* "We cannot make another person change [their] steps to an old dance, but if we change our own steps, the dance no longer can continue in the same predictable pattern."

A little background: When I say *attachment injury,* I'm referring to a time when someone in the relationship got the message from their partner that they were not ARE (accessible, responsive, and emotionally engaged) when it really counted. This sounds like, "I really needed you and you weren't there for me." *Early attachment wound* refers to repeated attachment injuries that we experienced as products of imperfect parents. The terms *enduring vulnerabilities* and *attachment style* refer to how early wounds show up in adulthood. According to the founder of Emotionally Focused Therapy, Sue Johnson, the two most common enduring vulnerabilities are 1) feeling emotionally deprived (starved, neglected) and 2) feeling emotionally deserted (abandoned, rejected).

I teach clients working with me to ask each other, "What are we *really* talking about here?" Sure, sometimes we really are just arguing about a busted dishwasher. Other times, the present conflict is actually something deeper coming up from the depths to ask for healing.

Goals

Begin to map your attachment injuries and early wounds.

Disrupt conflict by 1) asking, "What are we *really* talking about here?" and 2) identifying on the map where feelings are coming from.

Prep Questions

✶ When in *this* relationship have I felt alone or/and unimportant when I really needed my partner? What are some small, daily examples? What are the bigger, devastating examples?

✶ When in *previous* love relationships have I felt alone and overwhelmed? Are there patterns of partners not showing up as accessible, responsive, or emotionally available and engaged?

✶ What was the quality of my emotional bond with early caregivers? Were there any major disruptions (death, divorce, abuse) that left a lasting scar? Were there repeated experiences involving disappointment and unmet needs? Which kinds of needs?

1. Study my Conflict Iceberg image on the next page together. Take turns sharing about the hurts in each section of your Iceberg, starting at the bottom with "Early Attachment Wounds" and moving up. Outline the major injuries you've experienced and see if you can create a list of your enduring vulnerabilities.

2. Next, complete the following prompts and take turns sharing:

   Because of my earliest relationships with caregiver(s), I'll always be somewhat sensitive to _____ *(feeling deserted, feeling deprived, feeling inadequate, etc.)*.

   Because of experiences in previous love relationships, I'm particularly sensitive to _____ *(feeling unseen/unheard, feeling judged/criticized, lying, etc.)*.

   Because of my experience in our relationship, I'm especially sensitive to _____ *(sensing you aren't being fully honest, feeling rejected or inadequate, feeling like I am too much or over-the-top)*.

   It feels _____ *(name feeling)* to share this with you right now.

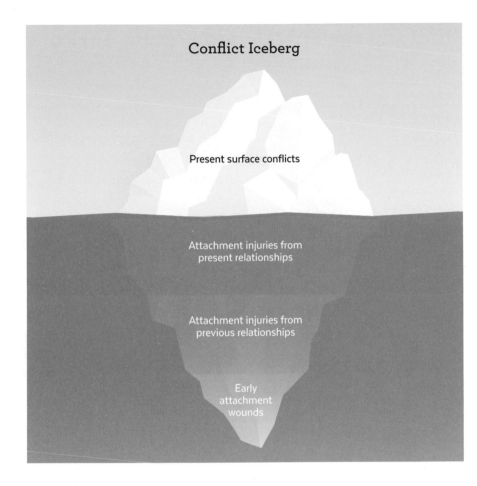

Conflict Iceberg

Present surface conflicts

Attachment injuries from present relationships

Attachment injuries from previous relationships

Early attachment wounds

Climbing the Polyvagal Ladder

FOR: INDIVIDUALS AND PARTNERS, SEPARATELY

What You'll Learn

* How to recognize what mode your nervous system is in and how to support it.
* How to use this self-awareness to set up you and your partner for easier communication.

What You'll Need

* At least 30 minutes
* Paper and pen or digital notepad for journaling

WHEN OUR BODIES interpret something as dangerous, we're wired to respond *rapidly*—automatically and without conscious thought—to escape, go unnoticed by a predator, or neutralize the threat. Very basically, we tend to do one of two things when faced with danger: mobilize or immobilize—hit the gas or hit the brakes. Understanding how our bodies react in this way can improve our ability to communicate with one another, especially about topics that could lead to conflict.

Here's the gist: Our bodies essentially have a gas pedal to gear up for danger and a brake pedal to calm down when the danger has passed. The gas pedal is called the sympathetic nervous system, or what you commonly hear described as "fight-or-flight." The brake pedal is called the parasympathetic nervous system.

It's only in the last couple of decades that we've begun to understand the science more fully, but we know that our longest cranial nerve, the vagus nerve, is highly involved in this circuitry. For our purposes here, you mostly just need to appreciate that the dorsal (top) part of the vagus is involved in shutting things down—like an emergency brake—and the ventral (bottom) part is involved in social connection.

Trauma therapist Deb Dana introduced the concept of the "Polyvagal Ladder" to more practically illustrate how our vagus nerve impacts how we respond to safety and threat. It's a tool that allows us to communicate what we're experiencing in our bodies, even if we aren't able to verbalize what we're feeling in the moment.

Goals

Being able to recognize where you are on the Polyvagal Ladder at any given time.

Begin to know what your body needs from you in each mode to feel safe.

Recognize when someone is not in "Green" and is therefore unable to do Safe Relationship Space.

The Polyvagal Ladder

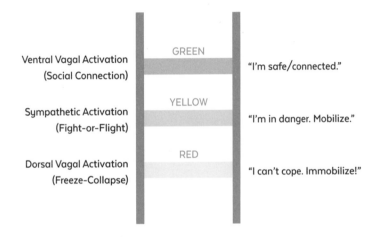

Ventral Vagal Activation
(Social Connection)

GREEN

"I'm safe/connected."

Sympathetic Activation
(Fight-or-Flight)

YELLOW

"I'm in danger. Mobilize."

Dorsal Vagal Activation
(Freeze-Collapse)

RED

"I can't cope. Immobilize!"

Prep Questions

✳ When conflict happens, do I tend to move *up* the ladder and react by getting defensive, yelling, pursuing, and/or criticizing? Or do I tend to move *down* the ladder by freezing up, shutting down, or going blank? If, depending on context, I do *both*, what seems to be the pattern?

1. Take turns sharing ways you can tell where your body is on the ladder.

2. Discuss how you can use the Polyvagal Ladder to check in with yourselves individually and to share with each other when things are stressful. Many clients who work with me like to use "Red-Yellow-Green" as shorthand for where they are on the ladder. If someone says "Red" during a conflict cycle, that alerts everyone that one or more partners will have to *do something*—on their own or with support from their partner—to "get to Green" before they can be present and able to engage.

3. Collaborate on a plan for what you'll try if *everyone* is in Red or Yellow. This could be showing a "time-out" sign with your hands and setting a timer for at least 30 minutes later to check in to see if everyone is open to trying again.

The Betrayal Cascade

FOR: INDIVIDUALS AND PARTNERS, SEPARATELY

IN RELATIONSHIP SCIENCE research conducted by Caryl Rusbult, John Gottman, and Shirley Glass, a number of factors shared by relationships dealing with RNVs were observed. The distinct pattern that emerged from their research is called the "Betrayal Cascade."

1. One person turns away or against a partner. A *turn-away* is when a partner doesn't respond or refuses to respond, aka: *stonewalling*. A *turn-against* is when someone responds negatively to a partner's efforts or *bids* to connect emotionally. Negative rumination (thinking on a loop) also begins.

2. Negative comparisons are made about whoever is doing the turn-away or turn-against (sounds like: "I don't deserve this," "Maybe the grass is greener somewhere else").

3. Emotional distance—the feeling that a partner is "not there with me"—increases.

4. More flooding or dysregulation starts to happen whenever negative events are experienced.

5. Repairs stop working like they used to, and a *conflict-absorbing* state takes over.

What You'll Learn

* A common pattern for how RNVs tend to happen.

* Ways to recognize and avoid the path toward violating relationship norms.

What You'll Need

* Paper and pen or digital notepad for journaling

6. A cycle emerges: more blowups lead to more conflict avoidance (due to fear of or exhaustion by the blowups) and more negative feelings get suppressed.

7. There is more avoidance of self-disclosure and vulnerability. Secrets or deception may begin here.

8. Bids for connection decrease.

9. Loneliness increases, while investment in the relationship decreases.

10. Healthy dependency in the relationship decreases; confiding in others increases.

11. Healthy sacrificing decreases and *substituting* (looking elsewhere to find what's lacking) increases.

12. Defensiveness and maximizing a partner's negative traits increases.

13. Minimizing positivity (downplaying the good stuff) occurs.

14. Verbal *trashing* of a partner increases and *cherishing* decreases.

15. Trashing of a partner to others increases and the "Story of Us" turns negative.

16. Resentment builds and a partner begins to be seen as selfish. Stonewalling increases.

17. Loneliness and vulnerability to other relationships increase.

18. Sexual desire decreases.

19. Pro-relationship attitudes diminish.

20. Innocent new secret liaisons begin.

21. Walls are put up between the self and partner.

22. Secrets and deception increase.

23. Actively turning to another/others outside of the relationship, either to fulfill needs or to seek what's not perceived as accessible in the relationship, increases.

24. Deception occurs and boundaries are crossed. Relational norms are fully violated.

Familiarizing ourselves with this pattern can help those of us who have experienced or engaged in RNVs to feel less alone and increase self-compassion. It can also help us to keep our radars hot in the future to spot risk factors that can push us back toward the danger zone.

Remember: The emotional landscape of our relationship doesn't *make* us violate relational norms—we choose to do that. At the same time, there can be factors that increase the likelihood that we won't stop ourselves when an opportunity to violate norms presents itself.

Goals

Be able to identify some parts of the Betrayal Cascade.

Begin to understand what sets relationships up for increased likelihood of RNVs.

Recognize that RNVs don't typically happen out of the blue or because someone is "bad."

Prep Questions

✳ When did I first notice that I/my partner was beginning to travel down the cascade? At the time, what did I not fully realize?

✳ If I violated lower-level relationship norms, can I give myself any credit or self-compassion for getting off the ride before engaging in a full-blown RNV? If I did go all the way to an RNV, looking back, where could I have gotten off the ride?

* If my partner violated relationship norms, knowing what I know now about the Cascade pattern, what would be some red flags to be mindful of in the future? Did I ignore flags before?

Instructions

Fill in the blanks of the following statements:

While we recognize there's no RNV inoculation or perfect preventative, we know that we can reduce our risk for being set up for RNVs by committing to the following 3 to 5 things: _____, _____, _____, _____, and _____ *(refusing to verbally trash each other, especially with people outside our relationship)*.

If one of us notices ourselves starting down the Cascade, we'll name it by _____ *(disclosing at weekly check-in)*.

We'll do the following things to protect our relationship: _____ *(co-decide to further limit contact with affair partner[s], schedule an individual counseling session)*.

Parts Mapping 101

FOR: INDIVIDUALS AND PARTNERS, SEPARATELY

IN THE PIXAR movie *Inside Out*, different feelings are personified as cartoon characters. Sadness is an adorable Eeyore-like blue character, Anger an explosive little red guy, Joy is bright and bubbly, and so on. All of these characters represent the different parts of ourselves that live inside us, kind of like a family.

It turns out, this way of thinking about all the different parts of ourselves as one family—our *internal family system*—lines up with the way therapist Richard Schwartz, the founder of IFS, was hearing clients in crisis describe different "parts" of themselves as wanting conflicting things.

When we are our *core selves*—which you can recognize when you're feeling what IFS therapists call the "8 Cs of Self": Clarity, Compassion, Courage, Confidence, Curiosity, Creativity, Calmness, and Connectedness—that's when we're most able to communicate authentically with partners and make decisions we won't end up regretting. When we have an awareness of what's happening inside of us so we can show up as our core self, we call it being in *self-leadership*.

When we're exhausted, hopeless, afraid, unsure, or otherwise off-balance, that's when it's toughest to stay in self-leadership. When we're in self-leadership, all parts of us are welcome and brought safely under our wing.

These parts come in two main varieties: vulnerable and protector. The vulnerable parts are "exiles" because they're often born when we experience a feeling we

What You'll Learn

* A way to understand yourself based on Internal Family Systems therapy (IFS).

* How to begin using the IFS technique of "speaking for parts" of yourself to express feelings in a way that can be easier for partners to hear.

What You'll Need

* 1 hour or more (Individually, up to a few hours might be preferred to prep for those who are internal processors)

* Paper and pen or digital notepad for journaling

never want to feel again, such as fear, loneliness, shame, grief, or rage. Protector parts—called "managers" and "firefighters"—are there to make sure we don't feel the emotional experiences of the vulnerable parts. One set works day-to-day under normal circumstances ("managers"), like self-critical or perfectionist parts for example, and the other kicks in automatically when managers aren't able to keep us from feeling vulnerable ("firefighters"), such as addictions or obsessions and compulsions.

When we have a map of our parts, it's easier for partners to hear us without taking things personally. Instead of saying, "I don't trust you," we can share with more precision: "My detective part, born during your RNV, is giving me a hard time when I try to access my trusting parts right now." With this tool we can also begin to learn how much of the reassurance we need will come from our partner, and how much we need to give ourselves.

Goals

Begin to identify, map, and "speak for" the three kinds of parts of yourself.

Start to recognize which parts took over in ways that set you up for the RNV and its aftermath.

Prep Questions

* When can I remember feeling, "One part of me wants x but another wants y?" (This is known as *polarized parts* and often occurs when we feel most distressed or torn about something.)

Instructions

1. Take a look at the Internal Family Bus image. The words listed to the right of the bus are examples of common "parts"; feel free to come up with your own.

Internal Family Bus
*based on IFS model of Richard Schwartz

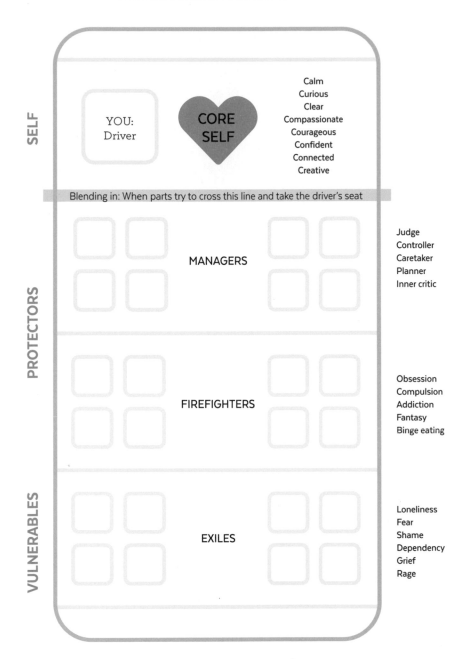

SELF

YOU: Driver

CORE SELF

Calm
Curious
Clear
Compassionate
Courageous
Confident
Connected
Creative

Blending in: When parts try to cross this line and take the driver's seat

PROTECTORS

MANAGERS

Judge
Controller
Caretaker
Planner
Inner critic

FIREFIGHTERS

Obsession
Compulsion
Addiction
Fantasy
Binge eating

VULNERABLES

EXILES

Loneliness
Fear
Shame
Dependency
Grief
Rage

2. Draw or list the different groups and begin to identify which parts of you exist. A part can be described like, "my anxious part," or "my anxious six-year-old." Sometimes parts have a specific age and look, while other times they're more general.

3. Take turns sharing how it felt to think about this and the list of parts you've become aware of inside yourself. Take turns answering: "Knowing your partner the way you do, what makes sense to you about their internal family and how it looks on the bus?"

4. Next, complete the following prompts individually, then share aloud together:

    The parts of me I like the most and have the easiest time relating to include: _____. The parts of me that I sometimes see as contributing to problems with us include: _____.
    It feels _____ to share this.

    I'm aware that the following protector parts were born specifically to help me deal with the RNV: _____ (detective, sneak, liar, gaslighter). Parts of me that were born to help cope in earlier relationships that got stirred up by the RNV(s) include: _____ (investigator, interrogator, debate team part, martyr, punisher).

    If I'm really distressed or dysregulated, it's often when the _____ (scared, unsure) parts of me want _____ (to stay in the relationship), and the _____ (enraged) parts of me want _____ (to leave the relationship without hesitating).

    In order for me to trust myself and show up for our relationship authentically, I'll need to focus on being in self-leadership of the following parts: _____ (denier, manipulator, detective).

Understanding Attachment Moves

FOR: INDIVIDUALS AND PARTNERS, SEPARATELY

THERE'S A PART in our brains called the *nucleus accumbens* which can influence how we respond to things in our environment, depending on context and how safe we feel. Sometimes it may cause us to move toward things in our environment with a sense of openness and curiosity. At other times, it may cause us to move away with fight, flight, freeze, or fawning responses.

We also have our attachment wiring, which tries to help us make predictions about our world in an effort to keep us safe *and* emotionally connected. You can review the four attachment styles on page 19. Each attachment style is associated with particular default tendencies when it comes to the way people respond to conflict or feelings of vulnerability:

People with "secure" attachment styles were nurtured in relatively optimal conditions. For the most part, their primary needs were consistently met by predictable and dependable caregivers who made them feel cared for. As adults their default tendency is toward interdependence. For them, it's comfortable to be alone *and* socially engaged, to trust and rely on the self *and* depend on others in a healthy way.

People with "anxious" attachment styles are specialized for over-stimulation. Because they had caregivers who tended to meet their distress with an increase in their own dysregulation, they learned early on to keep their radar hot, checking their relationships often to adapt to shifting moods and needs ("I'm responsible

What You'll Learn

* How to recognize when someone is asking, "ARE you there for me?"

* How to recognize "Pursue-Withdraw" relationship dynamics.

What You'll Need

* 30 minutes or more

* Paper and pen or digital notepad for journaling

for others' feelings and need to continuously analyze everything to be prepared for worst-case"). For them, it feels easiest to move from being alone to connecting with others, and their default tendency is to move toward people during times of conflict (pursue, persuade, push, reach, question, interrogate, prod, criticize, cling).

People with "avoidant" attachment styles are specialized for under-stimulation. Because their caregivers typically met their distress by dismissing, denying, downplaying, or shaming them, they learned early on to focus on themselves and not look to others for regulation. For them, it feels easiest to move from connecting with others to being alone, and their default tendency is to move away from people during times of conflict (withdraw, shut down, run, hide, stuff, dismiss, down-play, ignore, lash out).

People with "disorganized" styles of attachment are specialized for both under- and over-stimulation as well as chaos/danger. Because they had caregivers who were often unpredictable, scary, or even harm-ful, they learned early on that other people are dangerous and terrifying, and that it is unsafe to trust. For them, different factors may influence when they want to go from being alone to connecting, or from connect-ing to being alone. Their default tendency during times of conflict is a mix of move-toward and move-away maneuvers, depending on con-text cues.

Goals

Be able to describe the main ways you "move"—emotionally and physically—when you're feeling vulnerable and/or during conflict.

Understand why we move in the ways we do when we're either dysregulated and flooded or grounded and regulated.

Prep Questions

⁎ What were my main moves (toward, away, or both) during stress and conflict as a kid? Which of these am I most likely to still do sometimes?

⁎ In the wake of the RNV disclosure/discovery, have my moves been different or dialed up?

Instructions

Complete the prompts below individually and then share with your partner.

I tend to move _____ (toward/away) when I see/hear _____ during our conflict cycle.

In general, if I'm feeling activated or angry, I move _____ (toward/ away from) my partner by _____ (yelling, running away, criticizing, pursuing).

In general, if I'm feeling frozen/shut down/low/sad, I move _____ (toward/away from) my partner by _____ (freezing, hiding, going internal, fawning, placating).

Transforming Defensiveness

FOR: INDIVIDUALS AND PARTNERS, SEPARATELY

What You'll Learn

* How to increase your ability to respond to your partner in a non-defensive way.

What You'll Need

* Opportunities to practice this skill in the wild

RELATIONSHIP SCIENTISTS AT The Gottman Institute have found that four main factors can help predict whether a marriage will stay together and flourish, stay together miserably, or end in divorce. These are criticism, defensiveness, contempt, and stonewalling (not responding). Dr. Gottman calls them the Four Horsemen of the Apocalypse.

In the wake of an RNV(s), it's normal to see *all four* of these factors increase. This tool focuses on defensiveness, which can significantly block movement throughout the trust-recovery process.

In trust-recovery work, two general flavors of defensiveness show up: 1) involved partners not wanting to be seen as fundamentally bad, untrustworthy, or 100 percent responsible for the RNV, and 2) hurt partners who worry that their responses to the RNV will be seen as bad or unreasonable, or that they'll be somehow blamed as the root cause of the RNV.

If our partner is getting defensive, it's not our job to help them be in self-leadership of defensive parts, but our bond *does* give us a unique ability to help! We can do so by:

* Taking some responsibility for our role or impact.

* Avoiding starting sentences with "You" and sticking to describing *your* own feelings and needs and *not* your partner's.

* Avoiding words like "always" and "never" and black-and-white and either-or thinking.

* Showing "Same Team!" by listening and saying things like, "That's a good point" or "I didn't consider that before. I can really take that in—thank you."

* Demonstrating that we give the benefit of the doubt (if we do), as in, "I know you weren't trying to hurt me, *and . . .*" or "I don't think doing _____ makes you a bad person."

* Expressing appreciation by saying things like, "I know this is really hard and that you hate talking about feelings. It means the world that you're showing up to try."

Remember: If you're naming out loud, "My defensive part is starting to get stirred up" or "I can tell that defensiveness thing is happening" that's not *being defensive*. That's describing your internal world, which will help disrupt conflict spirals.

Goals

Be able to recognize and call attention to defensiveness without escalating conflict.

Practice shifting from being defensive to being emotionally attuned.

Prep Questions

* How can I tell when I'm losing self-leadership over parts of me that try to justify, convince, excuse, defend, dodge, persuade and reverse blame? (For instance, if someone criticizes us for not being honest, we might retort, "Well, *you* haven't always been perfectly honest with *me*.") What happens in my body? (Perhaps we get louder and more intense, or our "debate team part" activates.)

* When I honestly check in with myself about how solid my sense of self-worth and self-esteem is, what makes sense about why my defensive part is quick to leap into action?

* If my partner often responds defensively, would it be fair to say I could improve my ability to constructively share a complaint or request, instead of blaming or becoming critical? When my critical part moves toward my partner to say something negative about them, what vulnerable part of me is hurting? (My critical part shows up when I'm terrified my partner won't change and will hurt me again; my critical part shows up when I fear I'll go unheard.)

Instructions

For this activity, you'll practice working with a situation in which one of you is actively feeling defensive. There will be three general steps you'll try to take.

STEP 1: DIVING BENEATH THE DEFENSIVENESS

Defensive partner will start by sharing, or defensive partners will take turns sharing:

* When you see me looking or sounding defensive, deep down I'm most often feeling _____ (*unseen, sad, out of control, overwhelmed, judged/criticized, misunderstood, misperceived, insecure, self-critical, like "I'm getting it wrong," helpless to preserve our relationship*).

* When I'm feeling vulnerable this way, I can offer myself _____. You can help make it easier for me to be in self-leadership of my defensive part by _____ (*being mindful of not starting sentences with "you" and telling me what my feelings are without asking*).

Listening partner will summarize what their partner shared, being sure to repeat the *exact* words they used to describe important feelings. Explain why it makes sense to you.

STEP 2: DISRUPTING THE DEFENSIVENESS

Share with your partner what you agree to say if you become aware that you're getting defensive. ("I was just defending, let me start again." One client who works with me just announces, "Larry David!" to playfully reference a TV character who is known for being defensive.)

STEP 3: SHIFTING BACK TOWARD ATTUNEMENT

Agree what the next steps will be after the defensiveness has been named out loud. For example, once someone has acknowledged that they're moving toward their partner with defensiveness, they should stop and share a need. This might sound like, "I'm feeling defensive. Would you consider helping by being extra mindful to avoid words like 'never'?"

Sometimes our partners can't be expected to help with our emotional needs, but that doesn't mean we don't have a right to name them! For instance, an involved partner might say, "I really need you to believe me." That might not be possible (or smart!) for a hurt partner to do, so it's acceptable for the hurt partner to respond, "I hear you really need _____. I'd like to but I'm not able to offer that right now. How does that feel to hear? I know it's a shitty consolation prize, *and* is there anything else I might be able to do to help?"

CHAPTER THREE

Communicate to Connect

For me, forgiveness and compassion
are always linked: how do we hold people
accountable for wrongdoing and yet
at the same time remain in touch with their
humanity enough to believe in their
capacity to be transformed?

—bell hooks, FEMINIST AUTHOR AND ACTIVIST

I'D ESTIMATE THAT, in at least 95 percent of relationships I've worked with, clients initially tell me they hired me because they needed help solving a communication problem. "Communication problem," as it turns out, is a common euphemism for anything from "We don't touch each other anymore" to "We're each the loneliest we've ever felt and screaming at each other is the closest thing to feeling close we can get." Though it's these perceived communication problems that bring people to my office, the real issue isn't communication, it's lack of emotional connection and attunement.

In this chapter, we're going to learn to deepen active listening skills to increase emotional attunement, rethink our approaches to compromise, and practice completing a repair process to heal after specific incidents or conflict. While it might look like the focus here is on communication skills, it's *really* on connecting emotionally.

Mindful Relating Menu

FOR: PARTNERS TOGETHER

What You'll Learn

* How to make a complaint without criticizing.

What You'll Need

* The Mindful Relating Menu below

WHEN WE REPEATEDLY experience the same pattern of conflict, it becomes entrenched in our neural networks, and our reactions become fast, automatic, and unconscious. Once the pattern starts, it feels as though we're on a ship that's going down and we're being sucked under no matter how hard we try to stay afloat.

One of the benefits of having a professional relationship counselor is that we can help partners respond to each other in different ways (think of this as boarding a lifeboat) when the same old shipwreck threatens to pull you under. If you don't have a therapist helping to disrupt your conflict spirals, it's useful to implement some sort of structure to keep everyone from going overboard. That's where my Mindful Relating Menu can be valuable.

Mindful Relating Menu

Vulnerable Feelings & Emotions	Validation & Reassurance	Gratitude & Appreciation
Needs & Requests	Worries & Fears	Understanding & Empathy
Responsibility & Apology	Wishes & Dreams & Longings	

Goal

Be able to communicate with each other about a difficult topic without blaming or shaming.

Prep Question

✳ What do I most hope to shift about the way I respond to my partner during times of conflict? ("I want to criticize less and share about my fears and worries more.")

Instructions

1. When you're sharing vulnerably in your Safe Relationship Space, use the Menu to keep from spiraling back into your conflict cycle. Simply shifting from describing what you *don't* want to what you *do* want can make it much easier for partners to hear about our deepest feelings. The menu can help you do this because you can choose to share any of the items that are listed on the menu such as needs, worry, and gratitude.

2. "No substitutions" is key in being successful here—stick to things that are on the menu.

3. Agree that you won't take a "Gotcha!" approach with the Menu. If someone shares something "off the menu," just ask if they could give it another try, or say for yourself, "Let me try that again. I can see where I just went off-menu by doing the blaming/criticizing thing."

The Gift of "Of Course"

What You'll Learn

* What validation is and how to do it.

What You'll Need

* 1 hour or more
* Paper and pen or digital notepad for journaling

VALIDATION IS ONE of the most important emotional intelligence skills. It is about acknowledging that, even though we may go through an experience together, we can have different perspectives that are each inherently reasonable. We don't have to understand or totally agree with something in order to validate. Validating our partners helps undo toxic experiences of aloneness.

Validation is not just agreeing, admitting you're wrong or accepting defeat, saying that 100 percent of what your partner says is right, coddling, babying, spoiling, or giving in. Validation is when we give our partners this gift: "*Of course* you feel that way. I get it. Because I know you and your story, how you responded makes sense to me. You aren't crazy, irrational, or over-the-top. I get you."

Goals

Empathetically validate your partner about difficulties *outside* the relationship.

Validate when a partner is providing critical feedback about our behavior.

Slow down and validate during conflict.

✳ Are there parts of me that doubt that this will be helpful? If so, where did I see emotional validation modeled growing up? Did anyone help me make sense of my emotions? If so, how?

✳ Growing up, did I frequently get the message that I was too much or not enough? If so, how? Did a caregiver or even multiple caregivers turn things around and make it about *their* emotional experience if I shared?

Instructions

1. Look for opportunities to practice validating your partner.

2. Repeat back your partner's exact feeling words; don't just say "I understand." Instead try, "I hear that you're feeling _____ *(exact emotion word[s] used)* because _____ *(reason given by partner)*. Of course you feel _____ *(emotion)*. Knowing you and your story, it makes sense that you're feeling this way. I get it."

3. If a partner is shaking their head "no," looking displeased, or interrupting/repeating themselves when you try to validate, try asking: "Am I getting it?" "Is there more?" "What does it feel like I'm still not getting?" and/or "What do you still need me to understand?"

Listening to Compromise

FOR: PARTNERS TOGETHER

What You'll Learn

* Ways to get unstuck and shift back to attuned, active listening to set the foundation for compromise.

What You'll Need

* 30 minutes or more

* Paper and pen or digital notepad for taking notes

SOMETIMES WE'RE GOING to want and need things our partners do not want or need. This simple truth becomes more complex when what we require feels in conflict or in flat-out opposition to another's needs. Common examples in my office:

* One partner wants to open the relationship, another does not.
* One partner wants to get married, another does not.
* One partner needs to move cities for their career, another wants to stay put.

If we're called to compromise and it means we may not get what we want—or have a need met in our most preferred way, on our ideal timeline—we're set up for feeling resentment if we don't transform the meaning of the story. There's less risk of resentment if we know that 1) we won't be sacrificing or abandoning important parts of ourselves, 2) our partner will see and appreciate our work to compromise, and 3) any difficulty we experience in accommodating will feel balanced out by future rewards and benefits.

You won't be able to get to compromise if you can't effectively listen for and verbally summarize your partner's:

* Ideal scenarios
* Catastrophic fears and worst-case scenarios
* Deepest, core needs
* Longings, desires, and wishes

> ### Goals
>
> Be able to postpone trying to persuade and instead just *hear* your partner.
>
> Recognize when it's helpful to shift away from problem-solving mode and use dreaming and thinking out loud about ideal outcomes.

Prep Questions

* Did I have a healthy model to learn how to compromise? If not, what did I see?

Instructions

1. Pick an easy practice example.

    * Choose an example together of a situation that calls for compromise. Start with a low-intensity issue like what to have for dinner or what movie to watch.

    * Agree aloud that your goal is just to *listen* to each other with kindness to identify what is at the heart of the matter for each partner. This can help you start to feel a little less stuck even if you don't come up with a solution today.

2. Decide what you need most.

    * Individually, take a moment to list one or two things that are at the heart of the matter for you—the core needs that feel really important. (For instance, if you're choosing what to eat and you're vegetarian, a veggie option will be at the heart of your needs.)

    * Still working individually, take an inventory of the other factors that don't matter so much to you and where you can be more flexible. (In the dinner example, these could be that it doesn't

matter what time or where in the city, whether indoor or outdoors, or what type of cuisine.)

* The more you demonstrate a willingness to be flexible whenever it doesn't call for a hard-line boundary to get crossed, the more goodwill you'll build.

3. Listen for the heart of the matter.

* Invite problem-solver parts to sit to the side so you can focus on hearing what's important to someone you love.

* Take turns speaking. While it's your turn, share what's at the heart of the matter for you and list parts of the equation you can be more flexible with.

* Next, take turns speaking again and summarize what is at the heart of the matter for your partner (consider: If you couldn't compromise, what would they be most worried about or afraid of?). Validate anything that makes sense to you about what matters most to your partner. Why does it make sense that this is really important to them?

4. Find a compromise or agree to keep listening.

* If everyone feels heard and understood, brainstorm together: Is there room for compromise here? What would that look like? How would we work to ensure that any sacrifice feels "worth it" for the person willing to be flexible? How would we intentionally honor that flexibility if it is needed to achieve individual goals or achieve goals together?

* If a compromise feels possible, agree on it formally together. Here's an example: Say the hurt partner feels scared that the involved partner will violate norms at the gym again *and* the

involved partner feels ready to be trusted and wishes to return to the gym. The couple may agree that the involved partner will go even though it's triggering. They compromise by agreeing that the hurt partner will send a text to the involved partner when they finish the workout.

* If the compromise feels like something you won't need forever, agree how you'll let each other know if you ever want a check-in on it.

* Finish by expressing gratitude for your partner or their willingness to engage here.

The Three-Step Apology

FOR: PARTNERS TOGETHER

What You'll Learn

* A helpful framework for delivering a verbal apology.

What You'll Need

* 30 minutes or more

APOLOGIES AREN'T MAGIC spells. If you're trying to heal, it's unlikely that delivering words of apology is going to be *the* thing that creates some real movement in the relationship. Instead, in my experience, it's being vulnerable and *showing* our partner what's behind the curtain—the guilt, shame, remorse, and regret that's been eating at us—that causes a hurt partner's ears to perk up. I recommend focusing less on getting the words perfect and more on tuning in to the emotions behind the apology. This tool provides you with a three-step template for offering a sincere apology as well as nine things to contribute to a powerful apology.

Three-Step Apology

1. **Responsibility-taking.** Acknowledge and own how you impacted the hurt person. Take responsibility for actions that hurt your partner, even if hurting them was unintentional. Postpone any urge to explain that it was unintentional.

2. **Repentance.** Share about your internal experience of regret and remorse. Empathize with the hurt partner—not to feel sorry *for* them but to feel a bit of what they're feeling *with* them. Ask yourself: If roles were reversed, how painful can I imagine it being? Allowing a partner to see your authentic tears and sorrow can help more than words.

3. **Repair plan.** Specify how the apology will be *shown* through action and follow-through. Ensure that the hurt partner has a voice in the repair plan.

Harriet Lerner's Nine Essential Ingredients of a True Apology

1. Does not include the word "but"
2. Keeps the focus on your actions and not on the person's response
3. Includes an offer of reparation or restitution that fits the situation
4. Does not overdo
5. Doesn't get caught up in who's to blame or who started it
6. Requires that you do your best to avoid a repeat performance
7. Should not serve to silence
8. Shouldn't be offered to make you feel better if it risks making the hurt party feel worse
9. Does not ask the hurt party to do anything, not even to forgive

Goals

To use words to apologize and propose a repair plan, remembering that no one owes us forgiveness and that lasting behavior change is the actual apology.

Practice delivering verbal apologies based on the three-step template.

Prep Question

✶ Can you remember a time when you really needed your partner and ended up getting the message that they couldn't or wouldn't be there for you? Choose an example that everyone remembers and that was moderately painful.

1. Share with each other the examples you came up with individually as described above.

2. Take turns summarizing and validating what they shared then offering an apology with words. Use the following template for direction.

3. When you're the listening partner, let the apologizer know, "I accept your apology," "I forgive you," or "I still need some time *and* I really appreciate you taking time to apologize."

Three-Step Apology Template

I want to apologize. I'm so sorry I _____ *(specific action/behavior)*. It makes so much sense that you feel _____ *(repeat back partner's exact feeling word[s])*.

When you feel _____ *(vulnerable feeling: betrayed, alone, hopeless)*, I feel _____ *(vulnerable feeling: sad with you, remorseful, ashamed)*. I specifically regret _____ *(action/behavior)*.

I negatively impacted you/us by _____ *(reflect what sounds like the worst, most painful part[s] for your partner)*. I commit to do better in the future by _____ *(state your plan)*. Is there anything else you need or that I can do immediately?

Emergency Signals, Code Words, and Emojis

FOR: PARTNERS TOGETHER

THE WORLD DOESN'T stop when our relationship is in the throes of a betrayal experience—even if it feels to us like it does. While there may be some situations and events we can opt out of, there will be times we have to figure out how to show up for each other under trying circumstances. It could be that we have young children depending on us, extended family watching, or we're required to "show up" in a professional context such as a work event. In these situations, when full discussions would be difficult or impossible, it can be helpful to have some signals, code words, and/or emojis at the ready.

Examples of Signals

1. Physical gestures and actions such as making eye contact, pulling at our earlobe, or making the "time-out" sign

2. Code words or emojis that you can text or show your partner

3. Touches, such as squeezing your partner's hand three times, rubbing your partner's knee in a specific way under the dinner table, or tapping out the rhythm to a song on your partner's back

4. Innocuous-seeming phrases pre-agreed upon and appropriate to the situation, such as, "I forgot something in the hotel room" or "Will you help me with something in the car?"

What You'll Learn

* Ways to continue to reach for each other and communicate in higher-stress environments (family get-togethers, holiday functions at work, spaces shared by affair partners).

* How to communicate non-verbally with signals, to "name it to tame it" when the situation doesn't allow for processing verbally.

What You'll Need

* At least 30 minutes

> **Goals**
>
> Be able to let each other know—without words or with few words—when you need reassurance, co-regulation, or to do the six-step repair process (see page 102) together at a better time.
>
> Help keep each other from feeling alone in stressful situations.

Prep Questions

⚹ When I'm feeling stressed and overwhelmed, am I able to say words or a phrase to my partner? If not, or if it's really difficult, might I be able to use a physical gesture or touch instead?

Instructions

1. Working together, imagine a situation you might have to navigate that could be stressful for one or more of you and during which you aren't able to have an emotional talk one-to-one.

2. Decide together on a specific signal, gesture, phrase, code word, or emoji you can use to indicate the following issues:

    "An attachment injury has happened, we can't talk about it now, and we'll repair it later."

    How we'll let each other know when we're limited by environment: _____ .

    "I'm feeling overwhelmed/worried/scared/social anxiety, and I need you close. Can you offer me reassurance in some of the ways we've discussed?"

    How we'll let each other know when we're limited by environment: _____ .

"Someone with more power or standing in the group is negatively impacting me and/or speaking ill of us/our family. I need defending/protecting."

How we'll let each other know when we're limited by environment: _____.

"Code Red. I need to leave right now. Trust me and don't ask questions—just get me out."

How we'll let each other know when we're limited by environment: _____.

"_____." (Fill in the blank with anything you need to be able to name together. For example, "I'm starting to notice some of the signs our conflict cycle is starting.")

How we'll let each other know when we're limited by environment: _____.

Many couples like the simplicity of a "Red-Yellow-Green" system:

Red means "I'm/we're not good, let's go."
Yellow means "I'm on the verge, but I *could* get to Green if my need for _____ is met."
Green means "Hey, I'm all good right now, even if I look a bit uneasy."

If we go with this system, here's how we'll let each other know when we're limited by environment:

Red: _____

Yellow: _____

Green: _____

The Six-Step Repair Process

FOR: PARTNERS TOGETHER

What You'll Learn

* A structured repair process to use after experiencing a partner as not being accessible, responsive, and emotionally engaged when needed.

* How to shift from disconnection into reconnection after attachment injuries.

What You'll Need

* At first, you'll need at least 1 hour. With practice, the process will go more quickly.

THE SIX-STEP REPAIR PROCESS might be the single most important tool in this book.

Conflict in a relationship is normal and healthy. All relationships go through an ongoing cycle of what Dr. Jean Baker Miller described as connection, disconnection, and re-connection. Disconnection and conflict aren't fundamentally problematic—they're normal parts of human relationships.

It's when people show up to my office and say, "We never fight!" that I get concerned. Stopping all conflict isn't a healthy goal for a long-term love relationship. Neither, though, is kicking into problem-solving mode every single time there's conflict. Many of the problems in a relationship will actually be unsolvable, and a portion of those will fall under what's called *gridlocked perpetual conflict*—those issues that will be with the relationship as long as it exists. For example, one partner may be a morning person and one a night owl, and they struggle to have sex when both feel energized.

We will invariably bump into each other's enduring vulnerabilities and pain points. That's where the need for a repair process comes in. A repair process is not for bringing up general complaints to our partner such as, "You never pay attention to me." Rather, you do a repair process when there's been a specific incident or conflict. For instance, "We're going to use our repair process to talk about the conflict we had after the kids went to bed on Wednesday night and we fought about the clothes on the floor of the closet."

If, while you're doing the repair, you notice bigger, underlying issues, that's all right! You'll learn additional skills that will help with unresolved attachment wounds and gridlock.

Finally, an apology is not the same thing as a repair, but a repair often involves an apology. Repairs undo aloneness—they allow our partners to be with us in the present while we share how we felt that they were not with us in a past moment. In this way, repairs create a corrective emotional experience.

How can you tell when something has been fully repaired? For one, it won't keep getting brought up whenever conflict happens and partners can it discuss without getting distressed or lost in conflict.

Goals

Be able to soothe and reassure one another when an attachment injury and/or conflict cycle has happened.

Continue to turn toward each other vulnerably even when things are hard.

Prep Questions

* What did I learn about making repairs growing up? Did I see caregivers model this skill with each other? With me or any siblings?

Instructions

1. Plan a time to open your Safe Relationship Space to make the repair together.

2. If this is totally new to you and you don't have a therapist, set aside 60 to 90 minutes to start. If it feels impossible to communicate together in this way, consider enlisting a relationship counselor for support.

3. Agree that your goal is to nurture each other and feel even just 1 percent better in conflict.

4. Take breaks as needed if anyone floods, then gently try again. (Follow my six-step repair process described below.)

Morgan's Six-Step Repair Process

STEP 1: GET GROUNDED, GET TOGETHER

a. Sit face-to-face, eye to eye, or as close to that as your nervous systems feel comfortable with.

b. Ask "Process or Pause?" and check in with your bodies to see if you're emotionally available enough to proceed.

c. Affirm "Same team!" or "We've got this!" in whatever way feels authentic to your relationship. You can literally huddle up and high five if touch is more grounding.

STEP 2: NAME IT TO TAME IT

a. Take turns naming the vulnerable feelings you experienced during the incident you're discussing as well as those you're noticing in the present. Just list the feelings. Avoid the temptation to monologue or start blaming. Stick with "I" messages. *("I feel _____ when I see/hear you _____.")*

b. Describe yourself, not your partner. *("I feel devastated and betrayed" not "You're just a liar.")*

c. If your conflict cycle happened during the incident, make sure you call that out! *("That wasn't just a random thing, we did our classic pattern that we call our Doom Spiral.")*

STEP 3: IDENTIFY "RAW SPOTS"

The term *raw spot* is another way of saying trigger, enduring vulnerability, or not-totally-healed wound. Examples include feeling emotionally starved, abandoned, criticized, unheard, or controlled, to name a few. It's not our job to never hit a raw spot, but we should be aware and present if we do.

To help identify raw spots, complete the following prompts individually and then take turns sharing while the listening partner reflects and validates.

When I see/hear _____ , deep down I feel _____
(vulnerable feeling: sad, scared, lonely, overwhelmed, lost, worried).
This feeling reminds me of when _____ *(story of a time when you felt similarly as a kid/teen or time from your relationship's history).*

When I'm feeling the vulnerable emotions I just shared about, I need _____ . I can offer myself care by _____ . You can help soothe and reassure me by _____ *(giving me a hug and saying "I'm not going anywhere"; reminding me it won't always feel this hard).*

STEP 4: ACCOUNTABILITY AND/OR APOLOGY

Take turns acknowledging your role in the conflict, and if appropriate, offering an apology using the Three-Step Apology template (see page 98). Sometimes one person is more responsible than the other(s) and only one person may need to take accountability or apologize. For additional help, refer back to the Nine Essential Ingredients of a True Apology (see page 97).

STEP 5: RECONNECTION RITUAL

Choose a way to *show* each other through physical actions and/or words that you're on the same team. For example, you could each share two things you appreciate and one thing you admire about your partner, hug it out, or go for a walk and hold hands. Different actions might be needed depending on the context.

STEP 6: ACTION PLAN FOR THE FUTURE

Take turns sharing this statement: "What you do that helps soothe/ reassure me when I'm unsure/hurting/worried is _____ (*specific action/behavior[s]*). Next time we talk about this, *I* could help make it better by _____. *You* could help make talking about it feel better by _____. If the conflict happens again, one thing *I* can work on is _____. One request I have for *you* that could help would be _____."

The FNFL Rapid Check-In

FOR: PARTNERS TOGETHER

IN AN IDEAL world, we'd have time to do a full repair together whenever attachment injuries happen. In reality, sometimes we spiral out and there's not enough time to sit together for an hour and still make it to work or other commitments on time. In these cases, it can be tempting to sweep "small moments" under the rug, but strong bonds are built by threading together tons of seemingly small yet important moments where we give each other the message—through actions, feelings, and words—that "I care; I'm here; you're important to me."

I created the Feelings Needs Fears Longings (FNFL) check-in as a short-term bandage until you can handle the situation more thoroughly. This practice can also work for my beloved conflict-avoiders.

What You'll Learn

* How to do a mini-repair when you don't have enough time to fully reprocess.

* A quick, "good enough" way to attune to get through whatever has to be tackled.

What You'll Need

* At least 5–10 minutes and a relatively quiet area

Goals

Be able to feel even 1 percent better when conflict happens and there's not enough time to make a full repair.

Show up as ARE (accessible, responsive, and emotionally engaged).

✳ If I got the message that my partner wasn't ARE when I needed them, what was at the heart of the hurt for me? What might be at the core of the wound? Does the way I'm hurting seem related to something in our relationship, my previous relationship, and/or my early relationships with primary caregivers? How?

Instructions

1. Someone name aloud or say together: "FNFL." I have clients say it phonetically as "fun-full" because it sounds silly and helps them not take themselves so seriously. Plus, it can be hard to remember the list (feelings, needs, fears, longings) when flooded. Slow down as much as you can and check in with your body.

2. Go through this FNFL checklist individually. Take turns sharing your responses.

    F   **Feelings:** "I'm feeling _____" *(worried, lonely, sad, scared, lost, upset, overwhelmed).*

    N   **Needs:** "For emotional support, I'm needing _____ from you" *(a hug; to hear "I'm right here. We're going to figure this out together"; some space and to check in later).*

    F   **Fears:** "I'm worried/scared/afraid/terrified of/about _____" *(being left all alone).*

    L   **Longings:** "I realize deep down I'm longing/wishing for _____" *(us to be all right).*

3. Schedule a time to check in and/or complete a follow-up repair process, if needed.

Part II
STRENGTHEN AND HEAL

———

THE FIRST PART OF THIS BOOK was designed to help you navigate the crisis of Stage I by building safe spaces together to slow, stabilize, and allow anyone who got the rug pulled out from under them to get back on their feet. As we begin Part II, it's normal if you're starting to notice a readiness—or even eagerness—to address the *why* questions and move toward deeper insight and understanding. Once we're noticing signs of increased stability and de-escalation of the most intense negative feelings, we can begin to look at shifting and restructuring the patterns of our interactions together.

Trust, Love, and Intimacy

When a relationship norm has been violated, it's exceptionally normal for partners to notice changes related to intimacy. Some will experience increased sexual arousal and desire during high-stress times and others will experience reduced arousal and desire. It's completely normal if your relationship has felt:

1. more disconnection/distance and less intimacy and sex
2. more connection/closeness and more intimacy and sex
3. a combination or roller coaster of the above

Sometimes after an RNV, we'll observe an increase in two kinds of sex that partners can mistake for increased intimacy. These kinds of sex are what Sue Johnson calls "solace sex" (mostly a proof-of-love type of activity, more snuggly than erotic or sensual and associated with "anxious" attachment) and "sealed-off sex" (focused mainly on things like on aesthetics, frequency of sex, and simultaneous orgasm from penetrative sex as the only goal—associated more with "avoidant" attachment).

While it can feel dissonant or even counterintuitive that there's an increase in intimacy after we've gotten brutally real and honest after an RNV, it makes sense because bringing the walls down with transparency, honesty, and emotional attunement increases intimacy. Clients reflect back to me all the time: "We've *never* felt this close."

That's also why hurt partners do well to give themselves lots of grace in the face of the sociocultural pressure to label the involved partner with a scarlet letter or hear "advice" that says, "I'd leave for sure if a partner ever cheated." You may be seeing possibilities you didn't know were available to you because of the RNV. It's easy to fall more deeply in love with someone when they finally turn on the porch light and unlock the door to their vulnerability for us.

Remember: Sex and intimacy are not the same thing.

CHAPTER FOUR

Break Unhealthy Patterns

If I appeal to you for emotional connection and you respond intellectually to a problem rather than directly to me, on an attachment level I will experience that as a "no response." This is one of the reasons that the research on social support uniformly states that people want "indirect" support, that is, emotional confirmation and caring from their partners, rather than advice.

—SUE JOHNSON, THERAPIST, AUTHOR, AND FOUNDER OF EMOTIONALLY FOCUSED THERAPY

NOW THAT WE'VE DONE the work on establishing safety, gaining some self-awareness, and learning how to use communication skills to connect, it's time to tackle the conflict cycles and unhealthy patterns that can plague a relationship. Our main goals in this chapter are to identify and name your relationship's primary conflict pattern/cycle and learn skills to disrupt it. We're also going to focus on identifying factors that set us up for emotional disconnection prior to the RNV and practice shifting away from blaming and shaming when conflict does arise.

The main pattern that shows up in your relational conflict is what Emotionally Focused Couple Therapy (EFT) founder and master therapist Sue Johnson calls a "conflict cycle" or "dance." If you work with an EFT therapist like me, one of the first things you'll do is figure out what the dominant conflict pattern is and learn to stop it in its tracks so you can connect, attune, and bond instead.

Once it feels like you've teamed up to get a handle on your conflict cycle, then you can really feel empowered to work on some of the more insidious patterns present when relationships stop flourishing and start tanking.

Common big-picture patterns in relationships that struggle with trust and/or experience RNVs include:

* Inability to recognize/disrupt conflict cycle and do attunement antidote instead

* At least one emotion-dismissing partner

* Conflict-avoiding culture in the relationship

* High levels of resentment and a general felt sense of unfairness

* Imbalance of closeness/togetherness and autonomy/space

* Escalated conflict that doesn't get repaired but is instead thrown under the rug

* Pursue-withdraw dynamics and unprocessed attachment wounds

* Boundaries that are too rigid or too diffuse

* Lack of culture of appreciation/gratitude in the relationship

* Differences in sexual arousal and desire that are also undisclosed

* Low levels of self-worth

* Needs that feel voiced but remain unmet (a high-resentment scenario)

If you've had a betrayal experience, you've probably seen firsthand what can happen when wants and needs feel unseen or go unmet. You are probably also familiar with that regretful feeling that can come along with resentment. It's that sense that, had you expressed your needs in the relationship maybe you wouldn't be in this boat. "The terrible ifs" happen when we start spiraling into "What if . . ." and "If only . . ." or "If I had just . . ." territory. If you're noticing a lot of the terrible ifs, it can help to ask: "What am I aware that I might be feeling worried/nervous/scared/unsure/afraid about?"

As we start to take a deeper look into patterns and relational dynamics, I invite your most curious parts to step into the spotlight. If you hear an emotion word that sounds loaded—enraged, furious, frustrated, livid, devastated, abandoned—see if you can wonder about the soft, vulnerable feelings *underneath*. When we begin to listen for feelings, needs, fears, and longings, that's when we can transform conflict into a vehicle for growth.

One of the questions that clients find most helpful is, "What are we *really* talking about here?" It's just another way of asking the emotionally focused question: "ARE you there for me? Can I trust you to be **A**ccessible, **R**esponsive, and **E**motionally Engaged when I need you to be?" What's tricky is, if you didn't have emotion-coaching caregivers who supported you to learn to notice, understand, name, and share your feelings, it's unlikely you'll be in the midst of escalating conflict and say, "You know, when I see that affair partner keeps reaching out when you agreed to pause communications, I wonder if I matter to you. I wonder if you'll really be there for me or if you really want to be with her. What I need when I feel this way is to hear you reassure me that you want to be in this relationship and that you don't hate our life together—do you think you could help me with that?"

If you're laughing and/or terrified at the thought that you need to be communicating with the above level of nuance in the middle of the worst part of your conflict patterns, breathe out. Relationships really start to hit the ground running when they've had practice with three main things: 1) sharing their vulnerable feelings and getting validation and understanding from their partner, 2) identifying and sharing what they need (from self *and* partner) when they feel these vulnerable feelings, and 3) voicing requests and making commitments to try to do conflict better next time.

Recognizing Our Set-Ups

FOR: PARTNERS TOGETHER

What You'll Learn

* What sets your relationship up for conflict and increasing emotional distance.
* How to work together to manage/reduce/eliminate set-ups.

What You'll Need

* At least 30 minutes

PICTURE A LINE of dominos falling one after another. You don't look at the final domino and think, "Well gosh, I wonder how this ended up here!" because it's clear how each domino impacted the next. Unfortunately, when relationships experience RNVs, what set off the chain of events that ended in an RNV isn't always so obvious. However, we can work together to identify set-ups that made it easier for the RNV to happen. As always, we're not going to use this tool to condone, justify, or explain away RNVs. We're simply trying to identify factors and patterns we need to be mindful of in order to reduce the risk for repeating the RNV(s).

Some common set-ups include:

* Not finding a work-life balance; managing stress and burnout
* Not intentionally prioritizing time for one-to-one connecting
* Failing to appreciate and express gratitude
* Not sharing what's on your heart, especially if you're feeling lonely or rejected
* Individual partners not taking care of themselves and instead allowing their needs to go unmet
* Someone ending up feeling like a martyr with massive resentment
* Avoiding difficult topics and subsequently not knowing each other well anymore

* Increased exposure to environmental stressors (traveling with infants or in-laws) plus decreased connecting/processing time (being guests in someone else's space)

> ### Goals
>
> Begin to think about what factors set you up individually and as partners for distress, miscommunication, and conflict.
>
> Make a plan together to manage one of your set-ups.

Prep Questions

* When is it hardest for me to communicate vulnerably with my partner?

* When am I best able to communicate and attune? Why?

Instructions

1. Take turns sharing what each of you thinks sets you up for conflict. What often starts the ball rolling?

2. Agree on one thing you can be intentional about together that could help make it less likely that you'll spiral into conflict when you need to discuss tough stuff. For example, "We agree that before we open our Safe Relationship Space to do our weekly relationship check-in, each person will do something to get grounded first." Or "We notice we're less set up for conflict when everyone gets both enough sleep and movement (think biking, hiking, yoga, dancing, or anything you enjoy) in their routine each week to manage stress. We agree to prioritize getting adequate rest and exercise."

Antidotes for Resentment

FOR: INDIVIDUALS AND PARTNERS, SEPARATELY

What You'll Learn

* What factors set your relationship up for resentment, and what you can do to prevent/manage resentful feelings. We define resentment as bitter indignation at having been treated unfairly.

What You'll Need

* 30 minutes or more

WHEN I THINK about all the relationships I've worked with to heal through RNVs, there's one factor that's ever-present aside from lack of emotional attunement: resentment. Often, both partners are feeling it! Involved partners tend to have been feeling it long before the RNV. Hurt partners either felt resentment and did nothing about it (didn't choose to violate norms) or connected with feelings of resentment post-RNV.

Goals

Be able to recognize and list some things that set relationships up for resentment.

Decide on one daily way and one weekly way you can work together to reduce the risk for resentment.

Prep Question

* What sorts of things am I most likely to avoid that, in doing so, increases the risk for resentment? (Sometimes I fail to voice what I want because I expect my partner to read my mind; sometimes I get impatient or feel like a martyr and say "I'll just do it myself!" instead of allowing my partner space/time to complete a request I made.)

1.   Individually, read over this list of **Resentment Seeds** and make a note of which items ring true for your relationship.

*   Saying you're "fine" and not speaking up when something is on your heart or mind

*   Repeatedly hearing words (especially promises and apologies) that you don't see your partner back up with action or follow-through

*   Assuming compromise can't be possible and defaulting to sacrificing important needs or parts of self or/and giving ultimatums

*   Not voicing gratitude and appreciation, especially for "little things" that are part of the routine

*   Keeping silent about needs/longings/wishes to try to avoid disappointment or conflict

*   Turning away from partners or lashing out when they need and reach for us

*   Frequently giving up or showing up not for the purpose of lighting your partner's fire but to more selfishly try to get something in return

*   Leaving mental load and work-life balance unaddressed—perfect balance isn't necessary but a felt sense of "as fair as possible right now" is

*   Financial imbalance that is not communicated about overtly, such as one partner being the sole income-provider or having access to generational wealth

*   Unnamed or unmanaged jealousy

2. Individually, read over this list of **Resentment Antidotes** and make a note of which items ring true for your relationship.

   ✳ Speak up when something is on your heart/mind—don't sweep it under the rug or expect mind-reading from partners

   ✳ Back up words/promises/apologies with action and follow-through

   ✳ Intentionally, consistently voice gratitude and appreciation

   ✳ Express fondness and admiration frequently

   ✳ Notice and respond to your partner's bids for connection with you even if they seem small

   ✳ Share about individual needs and longings clearly and directly

   ✳ Pursue individual passions, even if they're not shared by a partner

   ✳ Talk openly together about power and fairness

   ✳ Do neutral-to-positive activities together on a regular basis

   ✳ Balance togetherness/closeness and autonomy/space

   ✳ Address the mental load and work-life balance

   ✳ Talk openly about jealously and fears about the relationship

3. Take turns naming one thing you claim responsibility for individually that contributed to resentment building up.

4. Decide together on one antidote you can do daily and one antidote you can do weekly to reduce the risk for resentment.

Mapping Our Conflict Cycle

FOR: PARTNERS TOGETHER

YOU AND YOUR partner don't have to be trained therapists to take a look at your relationship's unhealthy
patterns and think about how to address them together.
What you *do* need is a map that you can refer to
together when you start to feel lost or emotionally far
away from one another.

In this case, because we're basing it on Sue Johnson's Emotionally Focused Couple Therapy (EFT) and
bonding research, it'll sound something like:

*The more I feel an enduring vulnerability, the more I
default to a coping strategy.*

*The more I try to cope, the more my coping strategy
rubs your enduring vulnerabilities raw.*

*The more you feel your vulnerabilities rubbed, the
more you default to your coping strategy.*

*The more you try to cope, the more your coping
strategy rubs my vulnerabilities rawer, and off we go
into our conflict cycle.*

*It may go back and forth but eventually ends in
feelings of disconnection and distancing or separation before we come back together.*

What You'll Learn

- How to map and
  name the dominant
  conflict cycle in your
  relationship.

- How to recognize your
  conflict cycle when it's
  starting and after it
  finishes.

- The link between your
  attachment moves
  from and your conflict
  cycle.

What You'll Need

- 1 hour or more

- Paper and pen or
  digital notepad for
  journaling

That is the general pattern of how partners end up in conflict. There are a few common conflict cycles that tend to emerge over and over again, which—you probably won't be surprised to learn—are highly influenced by our attachment systems.

Some common cycles include:

* All partners move toward each other. ("The more I criticize, the more you counter-criticize"; "the more I defend and try to convince you, the more you criticize me and defend yourself.")
* All partners move away from each other. ("The more you shut down, the more I shut down"; "the more you go into your shell, the more I clam up and retreat into my head.")
* All partners move toward each other at first, then move away from each other, and finally one moves toward the other again.
* All partners move away from each other at first, then move toward, then move away again.
* One partner moves toward and another partner moves away.
* One or more partners sometimes move toward and other times move away, depending on which parts of them have been triggered in different contexts.
* The more one partner moves toward, the more the other moves away. This makes the first move toward with increased intensity, which makes the other move away with increased intensity and/or physically leave the shared space. (This classic "Pursue-Withdraw" dynamic is one of the most common seen by relationship therapists.)

Please note that it's normal to feel some mournfulness when learning some of these tools. It's common to think, "Maybe we wouldn't have had to deal with the RNV if we'd known how to stop conflict cycles and repair instead." Focus on how you'll move forward from here with what you've learned, even if you learned it the hard way.

> ### Goals
>
> Be able to map your conflict cycle and list your moves, which may have become a well-rehearsed dance.
>
> Begin to understand your and your partner's vulnerable feelings and the stories you are telling yourselves internally during the worst-feeling parts of the cycle.

Prep Questions

* When you're at the worst part of the pattern for you, what emotions do you feel? (loneliness, rejection, worry, hopelessness, shame, fear/terror, feelings of being overwhelmed)

* What story do you tell yourself at the most painful point of the cycle? ("My partner is just unreasonable! This isn't fair!")

* What story do you imagine your partner telling themselves about you when you're feeling this vulnerable emotion(s)? What do you think they see on the surface? ("They must think I'm crazy—they think I'm too much and that they probably wish they had another partner who was calmer. All they see is my anger and jealousy.")

Instructions

1. Take turns looking over your Attachment Moves tools from Chapter 2 together (see page 79).

2. List your main moves. ("I tend to move toward you until I get overwhelmed with feelings of helplessness and then give up and move away by leaving the room.")

3. Complete the following prompts together:

We can recognize when we're in our conflict cycle together because it sounds like this.

Name of Partner #1: _____
Name of Partner #2: _____

The more Partner #1 moves _____ (toward, away), the more Partner #2 moves _____. This activates Partner #1's enduring vulnerability of feeling _____ (alone, worried, overwhelmed, controlled), which makes them move _____. The more this happens, the more Partner #2's enduring vulnerability of feeling _____ (deprived, deserted, unseen, rejected, unimportant) gets activated and rubbed raw, which makes them move _____, and off we go into our cycle.

4. Complete the following prompt individually and take turns sharing with each other:

When I rewind a memory and freeze the frame at the worst part of our cycle, deep down I'm really feeling _____ (scared, sad, lonely, overwhelmed), even though it might be hard to tell because I'm _____ (moving toward/moving away) by _____ (specific move: criticizing, defending, stonewalling, freezing up).

When I'm feeling this, what I need to sense most is _____ (your emotional presence in the moment, space to feel what I'm feeling without problem-solving, etc.). You can help me with this feeling by _____ (giving me a hug; saying "I love you"; reminding me that it's okay to feel my feelings).

Managing Our Cycle

FOR: PARTNERS TOGETHER

ONCE YOU AND your partner feel confident that you understand the basic pattern of your conflict cycle, have a name for it, and recognize the feel of it, you can begin to work on disrupting it together! When you first try this, keep in mind that emotions happen so dang fast that you get credit for just noticing the cycle even if you can't yet stop it.

Once you've recognized the unhealthy pattern together, the antidote relies upon stopping and shifting into bonding activities that involve emotional attunement. Sometimes we can just stop and shift gears—other times an attachment injury has occurred and we must repair first.

Some Ways to Slow/Stop the Cycle

* Come up with a code word, or pet name for your conflict cycle so you can call out, "We're doing *that thing!*" or any phrase that describes how "that thing" feels (our dance, our cycle, the storm, our toxic tango).

* Use "name it to tame it" to describe: "I'm doing *that thing*," "We're doing *that thing*," or "I can feel *that thing* starting up."

* Pick a phrase like "Same team!" or "This isn't us" to express your desire to shift gears. Remember to *stand together* against the conflict cycle.

What You'll Learn

* Evidence-based ways to disrupt and manage your conflict cycle together.

What You'll Need

* 1 hour or more to share and brainstorm together

* Opportunities to practice this tool out in the world

* Allow yourself to be vulnerable and describe how you're feeling in the moment. Identify a trigger or "raw spot" that got activated and provide context by telling the story or memory when you felt a similar vulnerable feeling.

* Use "we" language to *ask* instead of *describe*, as in, "Are we doing *that thing*?" Ask your partner about their feelings/moves without describing them, and/or agree on how they would like to be asked ("Is that thing happening a little bit for you right now?").

* Agree on a physical gesture and what it means (when we make a time-out signal with our hands we know it means, "Saying words isn't a good idea right now, *and*—we're doing *that thing*.").

Goals

See "the problem" as the pattern/cycle, *not* us or our partner.

Choose two or three ways to disrupt conflict cycles that you feel could work for your relationship.

Learn to slow and stop your conflict cycle together.

Recognize when you need to shift gears and complete the repair process.

Prep Questions

* Of the ways listed to slow/stop our cycle, which ones can I see working best for me, even when I'm upset/defensive? Which things might *not* land so well during stress? Which of the ways to slow and stop might backfire or piss off my partner? Why?

1. Read through the list of ways to slow/stop conflict cycles individually.

2. Take turns sharing which ways seem *most* effective.

3. Take turns sharing which ways seem *least* effective.

4. Choose one way each of you can try to slow the cycle and one way you can try to stop it together. ("I'll name my vulnerable feelings, you'll name your moves, and we'll say, "Same team!" together.)

Primal Panic Protocol

FOR: PARTNERS TOGETHER

What You'll Learn

* How to plan for when everyone is triggered and dysregulated simultaneously.

What You'll Need

* 30 minutes or more

ONE OF THE tricky things about emotions is that they can come on incredibly quickly. To survive as a species, we needed to be able to respond to threats rapidly! *Primal panic* refers to the sudden physiological and emotional experience of our attachment systems alerting us to a perceived threat—this threat is magnified if we feel that the person or people who are supposed to have our back simply don't. Our bodies then suddenly flip a switch to "Oh, crap! Red alert! I am alone. I am not going to be responded to."

Depending on our attachment wiring, primal panic will look different person to person. Some folks will get big and loud, others will shrink and disappear, or we could see a mix of these responses. These default tendencies generally reflect how we were responded to (or not) growing up in the world.

Unfortunately, the speed of emotion makes it hard to catch ourselves *before* we've reached "the point of no return." I say that because it can *feel* that way, *and* research suggests the average person needs about twenty minutes for their bodies to return to a baseline state after getting dysregulated. So we *can* return—it just takes time.

As an individual, this isn't so problematic! It becomes trickier when we need or want to process with our partner *and* they aren't physiologically capable. It's like showing up to a friend's house and finding no one home—porch light off, curtains drawn, door locked. This tool can help us learn to reassure our partners when they're scared and we are too.

Prep Questions

* What do I need when I'm dysregulated? What happens when I get emotionally flooded? Do I tend to climb *up* the Polyvagal Ladder and feel angry and defensive, or do I drop *down* the Polyvagal Ladder into a place of shutdown and dissociation? What do I feel unable to do when I'm flooded? (Examples might include: say words, talk about something I haven't had time to think about, feel feelings, stop black-and-white thinking.)

Instructions

Fill out the Primal Panic Protocol planning template together.

WHEN

* Individually, signs that we are starting to flood include: _____, _____, and _____ *(thoughts speed up, heart starts racing, brain feels foggy, hands get shaky, "seeing red").*
* We will recognize we need to use our Primal Panic Protocol when _____.

HOW

* When one of us recognizes they're about to flood or are already dysregulated, we'll show each other our signal, _____ (*making the time-out signal; pointing to the red light on the traffic light image on the fridge*).
* If one of us doesn't recognize that they're flooding but notices their partner is, we agree to try to gently draw attention to the flooding by _____ (*asking, "Do we think that flooding thing is happening?" Note: "we" language tends to work better here, especially if anyone gets defensive*).

WHAT

* Once someone has indicated that we might need to use our Primal Panic Protocol, we will _____ (*set a timer for 30 minutes and go into separate spaces until we feel more grounded*).
* The main things that each of us really needs to sense or feel when we are all dysregulated at the same time are: _____, _____, and _____ (*to feel seen, to feel loved, to be reminded we aren't expected to be perfect*).
* What makes things tricky when we're flooded at the same time is that I often need _____ (*space and time, self-soothing*), which can sometimes feel in conflict with your need to _____ (*get resolution rapidly; feel heard and seen by me*).
* Sometimes, we'll just need to "name it to tame it" together and that will be enough to help us co-regulate and stabilize. Other times, we'll need to do a first-aid or full form of our repair process when we're no longer flooded if any attachment injuries occurred. If one of us needs to repair or hear an apology, we agree to support that by _____ (*scheduling time for a repair within the next 24 hours*).

CHAPTER FIVE

Restore Care and Connection

> We cannot make another person change [their] steps to an old dance, but if we change our own steps, the dance no longer can continue in the same predictable pattern.
>
> —HARRIET LERNER, AUTHOR AND THERAPIST

AS WE PROGRESS FURTHER in our work together, we want to move from a neutral place to a place where you and your partner can experience more feelings of joy, pleasure, and connection. We'll do this by identifying what habits *your* relationship needs to maintain a feeling of emotional attunement, creating rituals for partners to check in with each other, increasing verbal expressions of fondness and admiration, and finding a gratitude practice that works for you.

Check-In Rituals

FOR: PARTNERS TOGETHER

IF THERE'S ONE tool that clients working with me love the most (aside from the repair process!), it's check-in rituals. Having a consistent check-in is health-promoting for relationships because it reduces the likelihood that clients will get pulled into a conflict cycle in the moment because they trust they'll be able to share more fully about something during an upcoming check-in.

For partners who can hardly say two words without spiraling into conflict, their first goal with check-ins is simply to talk about the relationship without a conflict cycle. This could mean just sitting together and listing things you feel neutral-to-positive about regarding each other and the relationship. It's not uncommon for partners to fear that regular check-ins will do more harm than good, but the more times you feel successful together using your Safe Relationship Space to check in around big-picture and daily items, the quieter these worries will get.

What You'll Learn

* How to create a check-in that works for your relationship.
* Ways to maximize the efficiency of your check-ins.

What You'll Need

* 1 hour or more

Goals

Plan a check-in ritual together.

Think about whether your relationship needs a daily, monthly, and/or specific-to-the-RNV check-in. It's normal to need some that are general and others that are more specific.

* What's our schedule like? Realistically, how can we get at least an hour to check in weekly or biweekly?

Instructions

Go through the following check-in planning template together.

WHEN

* When will we do our check-in and how long will we schedule it for? (Recommended 30 minutes to 1.5 hours)
* What will we do if our usual check-in time has to be rescheduled?
* What kind of reminder (calendar alerts, etc.) can we use for our check-in?
* How do we know when we're finished? Do we set a timer?
* If one of us wants to request an unscheduled check-in, how will we navigate that?

WHERE

* Where will we meet to check in? Is there a special place at home that feels calm and quiet?
* If we have kids and/or share the living space with others, what factors do we need to consider for adequate privacy?
* When we're outside our usual routine (traveling, summer holiday, kids are home), how will we adapt to make sure we still prioritize checking in?
* How would we recognize if/when we need to change locations, specifically to go to a helping professional's office for counseling, instead of trying this on our own together?

HOW

*   How do we connect best when we need to check in? Would we be best served going on a walk to talk, for instance, or do we prefer sitting at the kitchen table?
*   How will we differentiate a general relationship check-in from a more specific, themed check-in (an RNV happened and we want intentional, weekly space to name feelings related to the RNV)?

WHY

*   Why are we deserving of intentional care and connection?

WHAT

*   What will our check-in include? (Sample check-in: We'll first share gratitude, then look at the upcoming week to let each other know where we expect difficulty and might need more support. Then we'll name any unmet needs we've noticed and make requests of each other, and finish by sharing what we appreciate about one another.)
*   What will be the goal(s) by which we measure the success of our check-in?
*   What are our rituals for initiating and closing the check-in? (We light a candle to start and then blow it out and we hug for 20 seconds at the end.) Most relationships that feel the most success with check-ins on their own outside of therapy report that they begin and end their check-ins by sharing three or more things they really like about each other. I can't recommend cushioning like this enough! Even when we're not feeling especially grateful, we can appreciate our partners for being willing to sit with us and try. The more heartfelt appreciations shared, the less likely a check-in is to derail, and if it does, it'll be easier to get back on track.

Practicing Gratitude

FOR: PARTNERS TOGETHER

What You'll Learn

* How to introduce a gratitude practice that doesn't embody toxic positivity, the mistaken belief that a positive spin should be put on all experiences.

What You'll Need

* 30 minutes or more

RESEARCH CONSISTENTLY DEMONSTRATES that taking time to consider things we're grateful for—without ignoring or suppressing "the negative"—promotes individual health and relational wellness. Healthy gratitude practices do not push us to "see the gift" in all pain, trauma, and suffering—that's increasingly being called *toxic positivity*. They simply help us to habitually make note of all the many things that are good and beautiful. Neurobiologically, this accounting of good, plenty, and abundance translates to our bodies as *safety*.

Sharing gratitude is also motivating for our partners. In relationships, it feels good to be seen for all the kind and helpful things we do that we're not even asked to do. Clinically, I see voicing appreciations really helps to reduce resentment. It's also critical that we let our partners know they're seen when they do things out of consideration for our direct requests—gratitude.

Goals

Choose a gratitude practice that's simple enough to do on a daily or weekly basis.

Use gratitude to cushion the relationship to make hard things feel less awful.

✳ When do I feel most seen and appreciated? Least?

✳ What was the culture around expressing gratitude like growing up? Was I forced? If I participated in a religious community, did any of those values inform what I learned?

✳ What are some of the things I do that I sense get taken for granted? What might my partner say I take for granted that they do?

Instructions

1. Decide together if you currently have the capacity to start a daily or weekly gratitude practice.

2. Agree on an intention that feels comfortable to everyone. See examples below if you need help brainstorming!

3. Make a note on your calendar for one month from today to check in and see how you've been following through with your intention. What will make this successful is consistency and repetition. It's better to do one simple thing every week than set out to do something elaborate that you only manage sporadically.

Sample Gratitude Practices

On a daily basis, each person shares something they're grateful for about someone at the table during mealtime.

Each monthly relationship check-in begins with everyone voicing gratitude. For example, start and end each check-in by listing three things each partner is thankful for about their partner or relationship.

Each person has a "Gratitude Jar" with their name on it and partners are responsible for writing at least five appreciations on note cards and depositing them in the jar by the end of the week.

Choose a community-service activity to participate in. On the way there, share something you're grateful for from your life. On the way home, share something you feel grateful for from the experience that day.

The LALA Ritual

FOR: PARTNERS TOGETHER AND/OR WITH FAMILY AND FRIENDS

WHEN PARTNERS END up in my office after a betrayal, they've often already been struggling with disconnection and distrust for many years. It's common for partners to report that, pre-RNV, they'd been living like roommates or siblings for years—solid at co-parenting but flailing intimately and relationally together.

A common factor I observe is that while they may say "thanks" here and there, they don't spend a lot of time voicing appreciations and sharing their fondness for each other's character outside of their functional role in the family.

Research shows that focusing on small things every day can help your relationship more than grand gestures. I made this tool for you to be able to use quickly and on-the-go.

What You'll Learn

* A quick way to increase the felt sense of fondness and admiration, which adds cushioning to the relationship for when we're called to do hard things together.

What You'll Need

* A few minutes to 30 minutes, daily, weekly, or monthly

Goals

Learn to intentionally keep reminding each other why you chose each other.

Follow through on building and strengthening a consistent habit together that helps build trust.

Prep Questions

* What drew you to your partner when you first met and/or when you fell in love? What would a fly on the wall have witnessed seeing you together?

✴ What about myself do I find fundamentally likable? Lovable? Adorable? Admirable? If that's hard for me to think of, what do I feel neutral-to-positive about? What do I accept? What differences do I notice in myself when I offer positive verbal feedback to others versus myself?

Instructions

Complete the following prompts individually and then take turns sharing.

L Something I really **like** about you is _____.
A recent, specific example is _____.

A Something I **adore** about you is _____.
A recent, specific example is _____.

L Something I **love** about you is _____.
A recent, specific example is _____.

A Something I **admire** about you is _____.
A recent, specific example is _____.

Feel free to repeat the same prompts, swapping "you" for "us" or "our relationship." This can help remind us of the strengths of our bond, our resilience in overcoming obstacles together, and times our worst fears didn't materialize.

Note: This ritual is an addition to and not a substitute for gratitude and appreciation habits. We're more likely to thrive in relationships if we highlight gratitude *in addition* to what we like and desire.

Internal Resourcing Together

IF YOU'VE EVER done individual therapy, your helping professional might have coached you through *internal resourcing,* where you use logical parts of yourself to take inventory of times you did *not* experience a feared or unwanted outcome and times you felt strong and capable, or at least safe and neutral. I've found that, for partners, internal resourcing together, or *relational resourcing,* provides massive benefits in terms of reassurance and grounding during stressful times.

This kind of resourcing balances our brain's natural tendency to fixate on "the negative." Our brains evolved to prioritize remembering negative experiences like the location of a venomous snake that darted at us—and not necessarily a beautiful songbird—in order to survive.

The goal of internal resourcing is *not:* "Let's ignore the bad and only focus on the good! Find those silver linings ASAP!" Rather, it's challenging our black-and-white thinking and acknowledging, "Yes, I cannot fully, safely trust yet. *And* here are some things making it safer to do so. *And* here are some examples of qualities and behaviors of my partner that I can put stock in."

What You'll Learn

* A skill for coping and co-regulating together when encountering a stressor or trigger.

* How to begin to reauthor your story together to support and rebuild the foundation of trust.

What You'll Need

* 30 minutes to 1 hour

Goals

Remember strengths that you can use to help heal and grow.

Be able to use internal resourcing during dysregulating times to increase stability.

Be able to reassure ourselves and each other during stressful times.

Prep Questions

✳ When have I felt able to trust my partner in the past? For instance, they supported me during a tough health crisis.

✳ What are hard things we've already had to face together and over-come? For example, we supported each other during a job loss.

Instructions

1. Reflect individually and complete the prompts below.

2. Sit with your partner and share notes and reflections.

3. Repeat this process as a way to meet needs for reassurance as you heal.

   Hard things we've overcome together: _____ , _____ , _____ , _____ , _____ .

   Times we showed up for each other even when it was challenging: _____ , _____ , _____ , _____ , _____ .

   Strengths we have as a relationship that help us navigate stressful times: _____ , _____ , _____ , _____ , _____ .

Times when worst-case scenarios did NOT happen or recur:

————————, ————————, ————————, ————————,

————————.

Things we do individually that protect our relationship:

————————, ————————, ————————,

————————, ————————.

Examples of new tools we have to help protect our relationship:

————————, ————————, ————————,

————————, ————————.

CHAPTER SIX

Deepen Intimacy

*The real voyage of discovery
consists not in seeking new
landscapes, but in having new eyes.*

—MARCEL PROUST, PHILOSOPHER AND AUTHOR

NOW THAT YOU'VE WORKED TOGETHER to build a strong foundation of emotional attunement, our goals for this chapter include increasing intimacy with a focus on how physical touch, sex, sexuality, sensuality, and eroticism influence intimacy and nonsexual bonding. You'll take a look into your partner's internal worlds to learn their wants, preferences, desires, needs, and longings and explore what sex and intimacy mean to your relationship. I'll also touch on how to discuss and express interest in intimacy and identify how unmet needs might have contributed to the RNV(s) so you can decide together how to meet those needs going forward.

What's Normal After Betrayal?

Clients often ask me what's "normal" in terms of sexual behavior after an RNV. The answer is that there's a wide variety. There may be an increase in sexual activity and intimacy, a decrease or complete absence, an initial increase that plateaus or stops entirely, or an initial decrease that shifts into an atypical increase. Also totally normal are an increase in emotional closeness and intimacy (even if sexual activity has decreased or stopped), or an increase in sexual activity with a concurrent decrease in emotional closeness and intimacy. In short, there may be no change, lots of change, or a sense of change for one partner but not so much for another.

It's also incredibly common for partners to blame the RNV(s) on the status of their sexual relationship. This is partly due to the myth that people only go outside their relationship when they're sexually unfulfilled. We can thank "emotional affairs," however, for evidence that sex is not the only thing that motivates betrayal behaviors. A variety of unmet needs can set relationships up for RNVs. More times than not, what's being sought outside a relationship includes:

* Accessibility, responsiveness, and/or emotional engagement

* Intimacy and a felt sense of emotional closeness

* Feeling seen/heard, prioritized/important, respected/admired, and/or treasured/special

* Freedom to (re)connect with oneself as an individual with dreams and desires separate from partner/relationship/family

Still, nine times out of ten during trust recovery, we do end up needing to do work around sex and intimacy. If there wasn't a shared, positive experience of intimacy pre-RNV, partners can learn to find their way to each other. If there *was* a mutually fulfilling sexual relationship pre-RNV, partners tend to benefit by exploring their emotional attunement and the structure or style of the relationship. It's common for a more-than-monogamous person, for instance, to have a fulfilling intimate and sexual relationship with a partner *and* to have needs that simply can't be met in a monogamous structure.

What's tricky is that reconnecting calls us to bring our bodies into close proximity in ways that might feel awkward or uncomfortable because we haven't done it in a long time. My advice: Don't go too far too fast. If you've heard that terrible folk wisdom that recommends you "have a glass of wine and fake it 'til you make it," let's go ahead and return that to sender right now. Enthusiastic consent and pleasure are what we're aiming for instead.

The Window of Tolerance

As couples are starting out, even just hugging for 20 seconds might be so out of the ordinary that threat-detection brain parts activate the survival-response systems. And this can be magnified if we're someone who has experienced trauma related to sex or sexuality more generally.

One of my main goals is always to make sure that we're taking on healthy challenges as we grow and change. It's a fine balance: We want to challenge ourselves, yet we don't want to push too far too fast because we don't learn well when our bodies are jacked up or shut down. Where we want to be is what clinicians refer to as the *window of tolerance.* It's that optimal state between being overwhelmed and anxious and feeling zoned out and numb.

How can you tell? If you're attempting an activity related to intimacy, sex, sexuality, or physical touch, and most parts of you are saying, "No fucking way"—I want to invite you to listen. That's your body saying, "No thanks, outside my window of tolerance right now." I recommend coming up with a code word and/or signal for "Whoa, we're exiting my window of tolerance. Halt action."

Here, again, a Red-Yellow-Green system can be helpful in communicating how you're feeling.

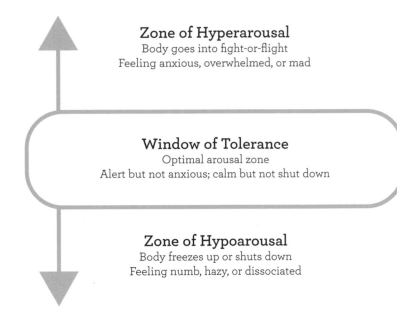

Zone of Hyperarousal
Body goes into fight-or-flight
Feeling anxious, overwhelmed, or mad

Window of Tolerance
Optimal arousal zone
Alert but not anxious; calm but not shut down

Zone of Hypoarousal
Body freezes up or shuts down
Feeling numb, hazy, or dissociated

Adapted from Siegel, D. (2009). *Mindsight: The New Science of Personal Transformation.* NSW, Australia. Scribe Publications.

One other thing to remember is that the window of tolerance can widen when we take safe, healthy risks that don't result in feared or unwanted outcomes. For instance, if one partner feels like they can't get undressed without getting pounced on like a gazelle in the Sahara, staging mini experiments where no initiation of sex occurs can provide experiences that expand the window a bit. The goal is to gently and steadily expand the window as it feels safer and safer.

A couple notes before we proceed. First, I'll be using the word "safety" in this chapter to refer to the felt sense of safety in a relationship and in our bodies that allows us to be physically and emotionally present and engaged in the world. Neurobiologically, I'm referring to our social engagement system being activated—that top rung of the Polyvagal Ladder. It can feel hard to hear that our partners don't feel safe in their bodies with us. That doesn't mean that you're bad or doing something unethical—it's especially common for male and masculine people to feel triggered hearing a partner report that they feel "unsafe" because there is a fear of being lumped in with abusers. I just want to remind us that this felt lack of safety often speaks more to the impact of trust and even to previous relationships and traumas.

Second, whether you identify as allosexual (you experience sexual attraction of any kind) or asexual (you don't experience sexual attraction, or when you do, it's not often or with much intensity), you can still use these tools to talk together about intimacy! Remember, intimacy isn't sex and sex isn't intimacy. A lot of therapists help clients remember the difference by describing intimacy as "into me you see"—it speaks to *knowing*, to emotional closeness.

Love Mapping 101

FOR: PARTNERS TOGETHER

LOVE MAPPING **IS A TERM** coined by relationship specialist John Gottman and used by counselors to refer to the intentional process of understanding—mapping—our partner's internal worlds.

If I ask you what a partner likes, who their best friends are, or which coworkers they can't stand, your ability to answer demonstrates the extent to which you've got an updated map of your partner.

During limerence—the initial six-to-eight-month "falling in love" period of a new relationship—all we do is love map. Super random fact about your boring niche interest? "That's the coolest thing I've ever heard! Tell me more," we say enthusiastically! But our brains would explode if we tried to keep up this level of engagement forever. Eventually, our brains develop a sort of algorithm for each partner, and we end up making predictions about them based on this map. Generally, this is really handy. The problem is that we keep evolving, as do our partners.

This seems obvious, *and* it can be easy to forget if we aren't intentionally reaching for partners with curiosity. If you assume you already know everything about your partner, you're going to get lost. We've got to have updated maps!

What You'll Learn

* What *love mapping* is, why it matters, and some ways to do it together.

What You'll Need

* 1 hour or more

Prep Questions

* In an ideal sexual relationship for me, what would I most want, need, and long for? What makes me most curious about my partner regarding intimacy and sexuality?

Instructions

1. Individually complete the following ten prompts for love mapping.

2. Take turns sharing aloud. If there's one partner who tends to shut down or withdraw, that person is invited to share first.

I feel emotionally closest with you when I see/hear you _____ (ask how I'm feeling, pull my body closer to you, share your vulnerable feelings).

In my own words, I'd define *intimacy* as _____.

I turn myself *on* when _____ (I've had enough alone time; I feel special and wanted). I turn myself *off* when _____ (I have a bunch of unspoken needs; I fixate on perceived body flaws).

I feel/have felt most sexually connected with you when _____ (we've had a romantic date together and come home to an empty house, we're in the shower together before the day starts).

As a lover, I want to be perceived as _____ (describe). I long to feel that _____ (I'm wanted; I'm still sexy to you). I'm sometimes/often (choose one) worried that I'll be perceived as _____ (describe). It feels _____ (safe, scary, embarrassing, difficult, relieving) to share this with you.

What really lets me know it's safe to let my guard down and open up physically/sexually/intimately is when I feel _____ (wanted, seen, important, sought-after, no pressure), which you can help with by _____ (voicing compliments, asking me what I'm in the mood for, touching me).

Something that turns me on just in fantasy that I think I may (or may not) enjoy in the real world is _____ (share example fantasy/fetish/interest).

If/when I masturbate, what I do is _____ (describe behaviors/tools/thoughts specifically). When we connect sexually, what's different from my solo experiences is _____ (name perceived differences: I can tend to get more in my head, I don't usually orgasm, etc.). It feels _____ (vulnerable, safe, scary, embarrassing, difficult, relieving) to name this.

Three things that I like that you already do when flirting/ initiating/having sex are: _____, _____, and _____ (specifically describe). One thing that doesn't really do it for me is when we _____ (specifically describe). It feels _____ (vulnerable, safe, scary, embarrassing, difficult, relieving) to share this with you right now.

When envisioning an ideal scenario, I think I might prefer to connect sexually about _____ (number) times per week. It feels _____ (vulnerable, safe, scary, embarrassing, difficult, relieving) to share this. If I had to guess what your general preferences are when it comes to sexual desire and frequency of activities, my sense is that you would like to connect around _____ (number) times per week on average. It feels _____ (vulnerable, safe, scary, embarrassing, difficult, relieving) to name this aloud with you. I do/don't (choose one) sense that we have a similar level of desire for intimacy and sex. It feels _____ (difficulty level: easy, difficult, super vulnerable, the actual hardest) to share this with you.

Offs Off, Ons On

FOR: PARTNERS TOGETHER

SEXUALITY RESEARCHER AND AUTHOR Emily Nagoski uses the language "brakes and accelerators" to describe how we come wired with a brake pedal (sexual inhibition system) and an accelerator (sexual excitation system) and everyone has different levels of sensitivity. Brakes and accelerators can be affected by anything we see, hear, taste, touch, smell, imagine, think, or believe.

Imagine a car in Park. Now imagine ramming on the gas pedal without taking it out of Park—can you hear that sound in your mind? That's frequently what it sounds like in the relationships that end up in my office. Clients have typically done lots of work trying to address accelerators—they've gone to sex shops, ordered a zillion toys, tried foods and supplements touted to increase arousal, and focused on trying to improve their appearance or performance. Unfortunately, none of these efforts will do much but add frustration if we aren't also shifting out of Park.

We need to turn off the offs *before* we turn on the ons. This simple concept can transform relational experiences and has packed more punch for me and my clients than almost any other concept.

This concept also helps us to work smarter, not harder. If you want to have more mutually fulfilling sex, everyone has got to have some interest in the kinds of sex available on the menu—if it's only great for one person, it doesn't mean that another has "low libido" if they don't desire sex. Here's an example: When I observe

What You'll Learn

* How to directly, compassionately identify and address things getting in the way of mutually satisfying sex.

* Which behavior changes to prioritize if you want to shift how things feel intimately.

What You'll Need

* 1 hour or more

male and masculine people trying to turn their partners on, they often focus on trying to be sexy—to look appealing visually and be seen doing impressive things. I can't tell you how many perplexed clients have asked why their guy has suddenly started doing push-ups near them while they're working or up to something around the house. When we understand our physiology better, we can appreciate that, for example, an hour cleaning the house to reduce one of the most common brakes—stress—for a partner can actually do more to set the stage for sexy times than an hour lifting weights to maintain a particular physique.

One other foundational concept related to sexual brakes and accelerators I want to offer before you try this activity is that sexual arousal and desire are not the same thing, and further, that there are different kinds of desire. For some people, physiological sexual arousal happens *before* a subjective experience of desire. For others, desire precedes arousal. For some others still, sometimes arousal precedes desire and sometimes it doesn't. The language for when desire just hits out of the blue is *spontaneous desire* (more typical for male bodies) and when desire emerges in response to stimulation, it's called *responsive desire*. No style is better or worse but, because we live in a patriarchal society, there's been a tendency to assume that female desire should work like male desire in spite of the fact that both groups are enculturated and trained in different, gendered ways growing up in the world.

Goals

Identify some of each partner's sexual brakes and accelerators.

Practice talking vulnerably and honestly about sex and intimacy.

Begin to co-identify some ways to remove brakes in the relationship.

- ✳ What activates my sexual excitation system? What are my turn-ons? This can be anything you see, hear, taste, touch, smell, imagine, or think.

- ✳ What activates my sexual inhibition system? What are my turn-offs? This can be anything you see, hear, taste, touch, smell, imagine, or think.

- ✳ What do I suspect or know to be some of my partner's accelerators and brakes? What are some I'm not so sure about and would like to get more clarity on?

Instructions

1. Individually make a list with columns for "accelerators" and "brakes." Write at least five of each, being as specific as you can. Remember to be kind. For example, instead of writing, "you not working out" as a brake, name an accelerator of "us feeling healthy and confident in our bodies individually."

2. Take turns sharing your lists. (If a partner tends to withdraw or shut down, they are invited to go first.)

3. Identify for each other which turn-ons and turn-offs are the biggest for you. (For instance, "My strongest brakes are stress and the felt sense of pressure to perform for you sexually and not let you down" or "My most reliable accelerators are being told that you want me and feeling your body close to mine.")

4. Take turns letting each other know how it feels emotionally to hear your partner's lists. For example, it's normal to feel sad or embarrassed if one of our go-to moves in bed turns out to be a major brake for our partner. Just "name it to tame it" together.

5. Finally, take turns sharing:

    * One thing you can do individually to help reduce/remove a brake of yours. ("I can talk to my doctor about birth control options so worrying about getting pregnant is less of a brake.")

    * One request you have for your partner that could help reduce or remove a brake of yours. ("It would really help if you could ask your parents to babysit Friday so we could have a private date night and manage the brake of worrying about the kids busting in on us.")

Self-Compassion and Sex

FOR: PARTNERS TOGETHER

YOU MIGHT BE surprised to learn that research on resilience shows that self-confidence is less impactful than self-compassion. That's right: it's not amping up our egos that gives us fortitude, it's giving ourselves understanding, kindness, and softness—grace—when we're faced with our shortcomings and the areas where we need to grow. When we can step away from judging, criticizing, and shaming ourselves in difficult moments, we're more likely to succeed at what we're aiming for.

In Kirsten Neff's self-compassion process, the main steps are:

1. Acknowledging the emotion/feeling you're experiencing
2. Connecting your experience to our common humanity
3. Offering yourself kindness in the moment

That might sound like this: "I'm feeling heartbroken and lost. Of course I am! It's human to feel this way. If I wasn't, I'd have to be dead or a lizard. I can offer myself some kindness in this moment. I'm doing the best I can and that's enough." If you're new to self-compassion, consider it a success if you experience acceptance or something neutral-feeling and notice a quieting or absence of harsh, self-critical voices. Sometimes we must learn to be neutral before we can be kind to ourselves.

What You'll Learn

* The basics of self-compassion.

* How to increase understanding and kindness for myself and my partner, especially regarding difficulties with sex and intimacy.

* Ways to explore and share about sexuality without blaming, criticizing, or shaming.

What You'll Need

* 1 hour or more

Prep Questions

* What is the story I tell myself about my sexual self and how it relates to the RNV(s)?

* How did I learn about sex and intimacy growing up? What did I learn?

Instructions

1. Identify some of the main vulnerable feelings that you're experiencing when it comes to the topic of sex and intimacy.

2. Take turns verbally offering yourselves self-compassion about the feeling(s) you shared. Incorporate the three steps listed in the overview.

3. Take turns validating each other. What makes sense to you about what they shared?

4. Individually complete the following prompts and take turns sharing:

   When I think about how I grew up and was/was not educated about bodies, sex, and intimacy, it really makes sense that I sometimes struggle in our intimate relationship with/to _____ *(Name the difficulty. For instance: "knowing what I want, much less sharing it aloud with someone else").*

Given my history in relationships with other partners, it makes sense that I move in the ways I do sexually because _____ (*Name the reason[s]. For instance: "I was taught in church that sex is sinful"*).

In terms of how easy or difficult it feels for me to emotionally connect with others and establish intimacy, the reason(s) behind that include: _____ (*Name the reason[s]. For instance: "My parents were authoritarian, and I learned not to express vulnerable emotions"*).

5. Now come up with a sentence together that everyone can comfortably endorse that takes into consideration the stories of your sexual selves and how you ended up disconnected. Think of it like relational self-compassion or *compassion for us.*

    (Example: "Of course we ended up struggling to connect intimately. Neither of us had parents who demonstrated physical affection toward each other, so we are working without a model. We were also both taught that having needs makes one a burden, so we honestly didn't even know what we truly needed from ourselves or each other to experience pleasure and intimacy. While we don't condone the RNV that happened, it's human that it happened and, knowing our stories, it makes sense that it happened the way it did. We were just doing the best we could with what we had at the time.")

Cuddle Puddle

FOR: PARTNERS TOGETHER

WHEN PARTNERS IN long-term, committed relationships begin experiencing a more mutually satisfying sex life, I observe a few common factors:

* Partners intentionally carve out, schedule, and follow through with private, uninterrupted one-to-one time that happens in a flexible yet regular fashion.
* Partners intentionally increase proximity by putting their bodies closer together and attempting to touch more in sensual and non-sexual as well as erotic and sexual ways.
* There's not an expectation that date night will necessarily lead to sex.
* There's not a scarcity fear making anyone feel like they have to leap at *any* opportunity and instead, partners can enjoy a diverse range of physical activities together.
* The goal shifts from focus on frequency of sexual activities to a wish for shared, attuned time.
* There's no pressure to define sex as successful when it ends in simultaneous mutual orgasm.

While I appreciate that many people desire an "organic" experience rather than scheduling time to connect sexually, we *do* often need to take a more intentional, structured approach in long-term relationships. For some, scheduling might always be a necessary part of staying connected intimately. For others, it might be a temporary solution as they find their way back to each other sexually. For some others still, scheduling might never feel right. Whatever suits your style, if you've never experimented with scheduling time together and you're feeling distant in terms of intimacy, I would invite you to at least consider it or give it a trial run.

I call this intentional, intimacy-fostering time "Cuddle Puddle" for short. If that's too cheesy-sounding for you, you can call it something else! I recommend starting with one hour of Cuddle Puddle once a week. If you're highly sensitive and/or have a low tolerance for physical touch due to neurodiversity or sensory processing differences and an hour sounds wildly unachievable, start with whatever feels like a safe challenge—even if that means a few minutes.

Partners can decide how they want their Cuddle Puddle time to look and feel, and it's okay if that changes over time. My recommendation: get as naked as you feel comfortable with and as physically close to your partner as feels safe. For some partners at first, this might look like sitting side-by-side in underwear holding hands. For others, a full course of sexual activity might unfurl with totally naked bodies. The most important thing is that no one feels pressured to do anything they aren't feeling. As Nagoski says, "Pleasure is the measure."

Goals

Practice bonding and connecting physically without sex expectations.

Increase physical closeness in a gradual, safe-feeling way.

Soothe threat-detecting brain parts and help them to interpret the partner and desired sexual activities as safe, even if they're new or it's been a while.

* Where do I feel coziest in the living space accessible to me? Are there any parts of me opposed to the idea of being intentional and scheduling physical connecting time together? What do they need to hear from me to be open to experimenting?

Instructions

1. Agree on when and how long to be available for a Cuddle Puddle. Be as specific as possible. For example, "one hour on Sunday between nine and eleven a.m."

2. Take turns sharing and validating any worries or fears that come to mind when you think about scheduling a Cuddle Puddle.

3. If anyone identifies a potential barrier to a Cuddle Puddle, share it! Listening partner, repeat back your partner's worry first, then ask any questions or make any suggestions you might have.

4. Agree to check in with each other after your first Cuddle Puddle. Make any requests for how to enhance or improve the experience in the future.

Sexual Parts Dialogue

FOR: PARTNERS TOGETHER

"Part of me wants you close and another part of me keeps telling me to run away."

"Part of me wants sex and connection and another part worries that being available for that will condone or reward unwanted behavior."

I hear clients "speaking for parts" of themselves all the time in our trust-recovery work. I invite them to do so!

This "parts language" allows us to reauthor the unhelpful stories we tell ourselves. Instead of, "I'm just not into sex now. I must be dead inside," we can say, "The vulnerable, betrayed part of me has activated my wall-up protector part. That's what's happening when I appear disinterested. For my sexual part to feel comfortable enough for me to turn myself on, the part of me that doesn't trust you needs time and corrective emotional experiences to see that you're emotionally safe."

This language also helps with confusing feelings like "I trust you but I don't trust you." It allows more room for, say: "The part of me that was born when I found out about your RNV—my detective part—that part of me still has a hard time trusting you. Many other parts of me *do* trust you. The parent parts of me trust you deeply— I'd never doubt you with our kids." Parts language lets us capture the dualities and paradoxes inherent in human relationships. For another common example: "I want you *and* we feel like roommates—my sexual and intimate parts deeply desire closeness with you *and* the vulnerable part of me that sees myself as bad has gotten a self-punishing part of me going. Part of me is so afraid I'll hurt you again it blocks you from seeing my erotic and sensual parts."

The more we can see our behaviors as part of a bigger picture and not the whole sum of us, the easier it is to believe in our capacity for change. "I don't want you to fucking touch me" can feel unreachable. "The betrayed part of me is terrified that, if I let you close, I'll end up feeling devastated again. It gets in the way of me connecting with all of the parts of me that crave closeness and intimacy with you" leaves room for more insight and pathways to deeper understanding.

It can be awfully hard to achieve something you don't believe possible. That's part of the reason I spend so much time letting folks know that I witness relationships heal through betrayal experiences all the time! I also want to say that I similarly witness people find their way back to their sexual selves every day. It *is* possible to have great sex again after there's been an RNV. It frequently ends up being better than before if you work hard together in the relationship.

Goals

Be able to "speak for parts of you" to communicate with more nuance and precision.

Increase understanding and acceptance of your partner.

Prep Questions

* How do I feel toward my partner sexually lately? What is it like when I imagine them initiating sex with me? What story do I tell myself about our current sexual relationship? What do I tell myself about my partner and why they do the things they do?

Instructions

1. Imagine that your and your partner's sexual selves are in a waiting room together. If you can, visualize them with your mind's eye.

2. Individually, write a description of what you envision. Where are the parts in relation to each other in the room? How would you describe their current relationship? How are they acting? What would they be saying (or not) to each other?

3. Describe what you would like to see change. (For example: "I see them sitting across the room from each other looking in opposite directions, totally avoiding one another.") In an ideal scenario, how would the parts be together? How would they feel? (For example: "I'd like to see them sitting side-by-side, looking tenderly at each other, holding hands.")

4. Next, take turns sharing your descriptions of the imaginary waiting room with each other. Be mindful when using humor. Your good judgment and knowing your partner will inform when humor might be helpful and when to keep your mouth shut.

5. Once everyone has had a turn, share with each other how it felt thinking about this and talking about it together.

6. Finally, if it feels okay, each person can share one thing they think would make their sexual part feel seen, safe, honored, and appreciated. Then, partners can help with the need if they're able. If the wish or need cannot be met presently, validate your partner's feelings about this.

Being a Safe Place to Land

FOR: PARTNERS TOGETHER

What You'll Learn

* How to show up in ways that support your partner's vulnerability so they can feel emotionally safe sharing about topics like sexual desires and fantasies.

What You'll Need

* 1 hour or more

WHEN WE LOOK at what sets relationships up for betrayal experiences, a wish to explore one's sexuality and deeper sense of self as an individual can often be found in the mix. Because so many cultures envelop sex in shame, stigma, and taboo, it can be normal for people to feel weird about sharing with their partners about their fantasies and desires to try new sexual activities.

For the record, we all deserve some privacy and don't need to share every single thing we fantasize about. To sustain desire, romance, and intimacy, we're called to achieve a notoriously difficult balance: space, freedom, autonomy *and* closeness, interdependence, and togetherness.

For partners to share vulnerably, we must offer a safe place for them to land. This means being open, curious, accepting, and confidential. A combination of these attributes builds trustworthiness and implies, "You're not going to be in trouble or made to feel bad about yourself for sharing with me."

It's also not the listening partner's job—the job of the partner receiving new information about their partner's fantasies and desires—to be perfect. We may not be able to help a look of surprise, for example—but it *is* our responsibility to understand and be mindful of our partner's enduring vulnerabilities and triggers and make efficient repairs when we inevitably bump into these raw spots.

This type of vulnerable communication can feel scary *and* it's worth-while. I can't tell you how many clients end up with regret because one person assumed another wouldn't be open to exploring something they deeply longed for, only to find out *after* the RNV discovery that there was and *is* space within the relationship for it. It's gut-wrenching to real-ize that, say, you went outside your relationship because you secretly wanted to experience a submissive role when your partner secretly wanted to be in a dominant one. The more our partners trust that they can be honest, the less likely needs and longings are to go unseen and unmet. That said, not all wants and needs can be met in every season. For instance, if you have kids and can only obtain childcare once per week, you might not be able to fully honor someone's wish to explore more-than-monogamous styles because you barely have enough time for one partner, much less additional folks. What matters most is that the needs and longings get brought into the spotlight, and we're not feeling alone.

Goals

Practice sharing vulnerably about your sexual wants and needs.

Increase understanding about what partners need to feel emotionally safe enough to share, especially when they feel nervous, awkward, or embarrassed.

Prep Questions

* If I'm going to masturbate or fantasize solo, what do I tend to think about? What is particularly sexy and arousing for me to think about?

* What worries and fears come up for me when I think about talking about sex with a partner openly and directly? What can I do to help steady myself in taking risks I've identified as growth-promoting, like sharing vulnerably? What could my partner do to help?

Individually, complete the following prompts. Take turns sharing your responses with each other. Be sure to validate as you go, to show you understand your partner.

When I think about a safe place to land for me, the main thing(s) I need to feel/see/hear in order to *consider* sharing openly about desires and fantasies include: _____ (*"knowing that even if you feel upset, you will work to not express frustrations in an angry way;" "hearing you say 'it'll be okay' if I get nervous or stuck;" "seeing you come sit beside me or taking my hand"*).

A time when I felt safe sharing something vulnerable with you was _____ (*briefly tell the story from your memory*). What I really loved most about how you showed up for me at that time was _____ (*"You listened without trying to immediately problem-solve"; "I felt like you saw the good in me no matter what"; "You let me just share about me before asking for space to talk about your experience"*).

When I think about worst-case scenarios in terms of sharing something vulnerable with a partner, the *last* thing I would ever want to experience would be _____ (*"seeing you laugh at me" or "having you be very quiet and unresponsive"*). This would be especially tender for me because _____ (*share a story that explains the source of the wound: "My family made it very clear I would not be accepted unless I performed traditional gender roles"*).

Something I've always kind of wanted to try at some point in my life is _____ (*a secretary and boss role-play, double penetration, group sex, having sex outside*). It feels _____ (*embarrassing, scary, awkward, relieving, vulnerable*) to share this with you right now.

When I think back on our intimate relationship before the RNV(s), it's more obvious to me now that, while I might not have expressed it in a way you could hear, at the time I was really needing _____ *("to feel desired and wanted"; "to see you also initiate sex and not be the only one initiating").*

CHAPTER SEVEN

Maintain Trust and Safety

> When our wounds cease to be
> a source of shame and become
> a source of healing, we have
> become wounded healers.
>
> —HENRI J. M. NOUWEN, THEOLOGIAN AND AUTHOR

IF YOU'VE WORKED THROUGH this book from the start, my hope is that the conversations and emotional bonding experiences you've had with your partner have increased the felt sense of trust in the relationship. Even if that means you trust just a little more—enough that you can talk about hard things together without spiraling out as much—that's amazing.

In this final chapter, we'll begin to reauthor the story of the RNV(s) so that it's one of resilience. We'll also identify ways to protect the relationship—by establishing routines to keep checking in, for one thing—and work together to create a container for the pain and heartache of the RNV(s) while agreeing on healthy relationship norms going forward.

Keep in mind that healing is not a point on a map, and it's definitely not a straight line. I invite you to release any expectations that you just put the ingredients together, set a timer, and ta-da—*there's trust.* Turn off the oven and close the kitchen! As author Ursula K. Le Guin says, "Love doesn't just sit there, like a stone, it has to be made, like bread; remade all the time, made new."

A past betrayal can be a bit like an old sports injury. Most of the time, you won't be too bothered by it, but sometimes it flares up and you have to slow and address it with TLC or professional care. I have a wacky shoulder from tennis but I don't consider myself damaged goods when it occasionally flares up. It doesn't stop me from doing what I want, as long as I'm intentional and take care of myself. I'd invite you to see betrayal wounds similarly. Certain events will cause flare-ups *and* it won't get in the way of life if you keep taking care of it. This entails allowing others—your partner—to take care of you as well.

"How We'll Keep from Going Back" Inventory

FOR: PARTNERS TOGETHER

What You'll Learn

* Another way of relational internal resourcing, or intentionally reminding ourselves of the strengths and positive attributes of our relationship when we feel uncertain and need reassurance.

* How to address worries that come up about potential future lapses.

What You'll Need

* 1 hour or more

WHEN A RELATIONAL norm has been violated it's not a matter of what to do *if* things remind us of the betrayal and our feelings about it, but *when*. As time goes on though—especially if you're being intentional in your emotional work together—it's normal to see distress and conflict related to the RNV decrease in intensity and frequency.

One of the main things clients report in terms of their confidence and ability to work together to stay out of RNV territory in the future is feeling that they can talk about issues, insecurities, and concerns, even when it's hard. It feels so much safer when we see we can trust that certain topics won't get avoided when they need to be addressed—that it's a norm to expect honesty and transparency.

If you've been working through this book from the start, then an important question to ask now is this: What makes you feel most confident that you and your partner can work together to keep your relationship in a healthy place moving forward? The thing that makes you most confident might be something you've seen or heard from your partner. One popular example: seeing a partner doing their own therapy and knowing they understand what set them up for the RNV(s). What gives you confidence in moving forward might also be something you notice in yourself! For instance, if unnamed and unmet needs contributed to the pre-RNV landscape, your commitment to staying open and honest with yourself and partner about what you're needing and wanting can help, and may already be helping.

> ## Goals
>
> Identify positive changes you've made and ways you and your relationship has grown.
>
> Recognize that there's potentially no foolproof way to prevent RNVs—no vaccine—*and* feel empowered by recognizing what you *can* do to steer away from RNV territory.

Prep Questions

✳ What's different about us since before the RNV? About me? About my partner? What relational skills and awareness do we have now that we didn't have when the RNV happened?

Instructions

1. Individually, think about all the work you and your partner have done to connect, grow, and heal. Make a list of all the things you've done as individuals and together that have felt positive and helpful. Rank them from one to three with three being most important.

2. Take turns sharing your lists. Identify any similar items.

3. Starting with things that everyone listed and continuing with highly ranked items, co-create a combined list that integrates each person's inventory.

4. Finish by reminding yourselves that thinking through "how we'll keep from going back" does not make your relationship immune to betrayal and RNVs. Keeping open the conversation that you bravely started together in beginning the trust-recovery process is what will help you most on your path.

Reauthoring Our Story of the RNV

FOR: PARTNERS TOGETHER

What You'll Learn

* How to intentionally coauthor the story of your betrayal experience to make it one of redemption and resilience (without engaging in toxic positivity).

What You'll Need

* 1 hour or more

* Paper and pen or digital notepad for journaling

WHEN WORKING WITH clients, I consistently observe that the story clients tell as individuals, and also together, about the betrayal experience gets co-edited as we go through the trust-recovery process. In the beginning, the story can sound long, scattered or complicated, and overwhelming. I often hear judgment, blame, and harshness. For example: "*They* made a terrible choice and betrayed me. *They* have to change to keep it from happening again, but they're out of control and heartless."

When healing has started to transform the relationship, the stories clients tell about what happened become shorter yet more powerful. Details about the affair partner or partners and how things went down tend to drop off. Fixation on the lying and manner of discovery eases. The discussion becomes less of a monologue and includes more "we" language. That can end up sounding more like, "We were doing the best with what we had at the time, *and* neither of us were given the tools to prepare us for emotionally connecting in a long-term relationship. We stopped being intentional and got distant. Instead of reaching for each other when the loneliness got unbearable, we shut each other out, and one (or more) of us violated our relationship's norms in an effort to ease the lonely feeling. Now we know how to reach for each other when it counts instead of turning away and losing our way to each other."

In *Daring Greatly,* Brené Brown reminds us that "When we deny our stories, they define us. When we own our stories, we get to write a brave new ending." This tool is about taking power back to define your reality for yourselves. It's about reclaiming your story together and making space for alternate endings.

Goals

Be able to tell an abridged version of the story of the RNV(s) in your relationship that everyone feels comfortable endorsing.

Increase felt sense of being on the same page and same team.

Prep Questions

* What's the story I currently tell myself about what happened with our relationship? Has it changed from the way I was telling the story in the immediate aftermath of the RNV, and if so, how?

* If you had to make a short movie about your betrayal experience, which scenes would you include? How would it begin and end?

Instructions

1. After individually taking time to outline the story from each of your perspectives, take turns reading aloud what you've written. When it's your turn to listen, wait until your partner has finished their telling of the story, then summarize it back to them verbally to make sure they sense you have an understanding of things from their perspective.

2. Practice listening actively without interrupting your partner or getting defensive. If you've heard something that feels untrue or

unclear, wait until your partner has finished sharing their version of the story, then ask any clarifying questions you have.

3.   Work together to weave your versions into one story that tells the tale of the RNV(s). It can be helpful to actually write or type it out!

4.   Finally, turn to each other and share how it feels hearing the story's beginning, middle, and end. If it feels like the ending is still open, share about the ideal outcome you'd envision. What might still have to happen for the story to turn into one of redemption and possibility?

Relationship Norms and Co-Agreements

FOR: PARTNERS TOGETHER

RELATIONSHIP NORMS AND expectations should be continually discussed and updated as long as we're in a long-term relationship. After all, what's normal and reasonable in one season of your life together might not work down the line. Doing this consistently proves helpful for the partners who work with me.

A common example of a critical discussion point involves boundaries around communication with other people—this is a boundary that can easily shift with time and repair progress made. It's normal for a couple to agree on a slightly different approach to privacy while trust is being regained. For some people, this might look like sharing passcodes to devices to increase transparency, while for others it means letting your partner know immediately when an affair partner makes any attempts at contact. As trust increases, we'll feel less of a need for super rigid boundaries because that out-of-control feeling won't be so overwhelming. Once things feel emotionally safe again, the need for higher-than-usual levels of transparency and detail can fade out and privacy can increase.

I invite partners to list positive statements that reflect the norms they agree to. Some examples of co-agreements include:

* We only engage in sexual activities with each other.
* We make repairs within one to two days when a conflict cycle results in an attachment injury.

What You'll Learn

* A clearer vision of what you and your partner agree are the norms in your relationship and what's reasonable to expect from each other and from the partnership.

* Why it's important to build habits around checking in and updating relational co-agreements as you evolve individually and grow together across time.

What You'll Need

* 1 hour or more

- We let each other know if we have a crush on someone outside the relationship.
- We don't keep secrets that could harm our relationship.
- We debrief together after attending an event where a previous affair partner is present.
- We get screened for STIs three months after connecting with any new sexual partners.
- We ask to do a Co-Agreement Check-In when someone would like to revisit and possibly change an agreement.
- If someone outside the relationship expresses interest in us, we disclose that to each other within 24 hours.
- We don't have additional play partners who are work colleagues or friends of colleagues.

Goals

Increase clarity around your relational values and norms and current co-agreements.

Co-create a list of agreements that feel most important to honor in your relationship so that everyone feels as emotionally safe as possible, even during hard times.

Be able to return to co-agreements and discuss wishes to edit, adapt, or cancel.

Prep Questions

- What are some important relational norms that feel like core needs for me (we're monogamous; we're more-than-monogamous; we make advance requests if we need to move our standing weekly date due to things like accommodating the other partner's schedule)? If I wasn't in a relationship where I could reasonably expect relational norms, would I feel in alignment with myself and my values?

- Are there any norms I would want to advocate for that I worry my partner might not want?

Instructions

1. Brainstorm co-agreements aloud together, making notes as you go for future reference.

2. Remember that you're making *agreements* together and not *rules*. The goal is clarity, not control. Try to describe what you *do* want rather than what you *don't* want.

   Co-create a list of at least five relational norms everyone can wholeheartedly endorse. This will be your working list of co-agreements.

3. If there's disagreement, refer back to the compromise and gridlock tools in Chapter 3 to see if shifting gears and thinking more about the underlying hopes and fears might help grease the wheels a bit.

4. Decide how you will let each other know if anyone would like to open the Safe Relationship Space to dialogue about updating, editing, or cancelling any earlier co-agreements that no longer serve the relationship. ("I will say, 'Hey, could we schedule time to look at our co-agreements together?' and make sure to let you know everything is okay.")

Agree to get your list "good enough" for now. If there was lying by omission as part of the wounding, it's normal if a hurt partner feels a need to be ultra-specific. I'd invite you to just notice your preferences regarding specificity—could it speak to your level of trust in your partner?

If you feel unable to engage in this activity without escalating into conflict or getting stuck in gridlock, or you've tried taking breaks and returning to it but keep getting stuck, that might be an indicator there are some critical value differences that will be hard to explore or overcome without the support of a mediator, helping professional, or trusted third party.

Balancing Closeness and Autonomy

FOR: PARTNERS TOGETHER

What You'll Learn

* One check-in format for building a habit of openly talking about the balance of 1) closeness/togetherness and 2) space/autonomy in your relationship.

What You'll Need

* 1 hour or more for initial conversation, especially if you're new to discussing this balance, and at least 30 minutes for check-ins (you can try weekly, biweekly, monthly, or quarterly, depending what feels right for your relationship)

YOU'LL OFTEN HEAR clinicians juxtapose relationship experts Esther Perel and John Gottman in ways that suggest opposition in their work and theories. They'll say, "Perel advocates for distance and mystery. Gottman is all about friendship and closeness." In thinking about how these two therapists support relationships, I think it's helpful to acknowledge that it's not an either-or paradigm at all. It's true that relationship research out of The Gottman Institute finds that friendship is highly predictive when it comes to whether relationships stay together. That said, any sex therapist will tell you that solid friendship isn't enough for a relationship to flourish. With this tool, we'll practice finding a healthy balance between closeness and space.

Goals

Prioritize *both* your relationship and yourself as an individual.

Reflect deeply on any unmet needs related to space or closeness.

Be able to share vulnerably with your partner if you have any requests for change.

✳ Am I getting enough alone time? Do I notice my partner supporting me when I attempt to take space to meet my individual needs?

✳ Am I getting enough support and connecting time lately? Do I feel seen, heard, responded to, important, and prioritized?

Instructions

Complete the following prompts individually, then take turns sharing your responses. Start with each person sharing their response to prompt number one before moving on to number two and so on. If you have difficulty with any of the prompts, name any feelings that come up. For example, "I feel sad that I'm having a hard time thinking of ways I've seen you pour into me."

If your conflict cycle begins, stop and recognize where you are in the pattern. Remember together that talking about this balance can be triggering because it involves awareness of unmet needs and longings. The feedback is not to criticize, rather truly to help improve your ability to meet your own needs and help with each other's needs where appropriate.

1. Some ways I've felt you pour into me this week include: _____. I'm so grateful for that. Some ways I've felt you pour into our relationship in the past include: _____. Those things mean the world to me.

2. Some ways I've tried to pour into myself this month include: _____. Some ways I've tried to pour into you this month include: _____. Some ways I've tried to pour into our relationship this month include: _____. Some ways I've tried to pour into our family or/and chosen family/community include: _____.

3. When I think back, examples of times where I could have done better include: _____ . I want to commit to working to _____ (specific behavior/action/follow-through).

4a. One request that I have which would help me feel _____ (loved, supported, cared for, nurtured, poured-into, treasured, admired, more trust in you) for this week is: _____ . One request that I have which I think will help our relationship is: _____ . Would you be willing to try this?

4b. Listening partner, you're invited to respond. If there's disagreement about the request, revisit the compromise, gridlock, and repair tools in Chapter 3. See if you can co-agree to one thing you could try that might help things to feel even 1 percent better.

5. Thinking about the *mental load*—everything that it takes to keep our life running day-to-day—and our work-life balance, lately I feel _____ (vulnerable, overwhelmed, hopeless). (Note: If you want to name reactive feelings like anger or frustration, make sure to claim the soft feelings underneath in the same sentence as much as possible). It feels _____ (easy, refreshing, relieving, vulnerable, difficult) to share this with you right now.

6. While we acknowledge we can't make things feel perfectly even and 100 percent fair and balanced all the time, one thing you could do over the next month that would really positively impact me in terms of the mental load would be _____ . One thing I can commit to working on to help us move toward each other and stay in balance would be _____ .

7a. Over the last month, when I think about whether or not I've gotten adequate space and alone time, I feel _____ *(good, disappointed, hopeless, distressed, overwhelmed, all right)*.
If I had one request related to my individual experience of feeling "enough space" in our relationship, it might be: _____
(having one night a week where I go out by myself with friends, joining separate running clubs, getting you to take the kids so I can go out for a solo coffee on Friday mornings). Would you be willing to try this?

7b. Listening partner, you're invited to respond. If there's disagreement about the request, revisit the compromise, gridlock, and repair tools in Chapter 3. See if you can co-agree to one thing you could try that might help things to feel even 1 percent better.

CONCLUSION

This life is mine alone. So I have stopped asking people for directions to places they've never been. —GLENNON DOYLE, AUTHOR AND ACTIVIST

IF YOU'VE FOUND YOURSELF HERE after working your way through this book, I want to share my most heartfelt appreciation for your time and efforts. Whether you did it for yourself, your partner, your family, or as a Hail Mary to try to save something precious, you deserve credit for meeting the call for honesty, courage, and patience. You've learned about the trust-recovery process along with a heck ton of neurobiology and psychology! There are therapists out there who know less than you now know.

As you might imagine, people I meet socially make a lot of predictable jokes about my work as a therapist and trust-recovery specialist. The one I have the least patience for is, "Oh man, you must really see the worst of the worst!" Actually, no—I do not. The people who sit with me are the best of the best, no matter where they've been. They are brave and resilient, fiercely loving, unbelievably patient, and full of mercy and grace. We might not have sat together in the real world face-to-face sense, *and* I hope you can believe I think the same things about you, wherever you are and whatever you're going through.

The ending of a therapeutic relationship is clinically referred to as *termination* (which I can never think about without an image of Schwarzenegger popping to mind). As therapists, we come to deeply love and admire the clients who work with us. There's just nothing more humbling than being permitted to walk so closely alongside folks through some of their hardest days. Goodbyes aren't often easy.

The most important thing that I want to send clients out into the world with, at the end of our work together, is a sense that they don't need me—that they can take care of each other more times than not. Of course, my door stays open, and it's normal to check in when there are big life changes. *And* I see termination as successful when clients express things like, "We got this. We've got each other."

While it's not lost on me that this book isn't equivalent to psychotherapy, my hope is still that you feel more competent and confident when it comes to emotionally attuning and communicating at very deep levels. I hope you might still bust this book out from time to time, *and* that you can lean into each other when things are rough.

Please note that if you've earnestly worked your way through this book together and one or more partners is still experiencing significant distress more days than not or you feel unable to stop your conflict cycle together, it might be time to reconsider therapy if you haven't already. Relationship therapists are like life jackets—even the best swimmers sometimes need to wear one when they are moving through dangerous waters.

Now I'll sign off as I do at the end of a session with partners working with me: Y'all take good care of yourselves and each other.

Morgan's Feelings List

HAPPINESS + CALM

Affectionate
Calm
Confident
Content
Easygoing
Encouraged
Fulfilled
Grateful
Happy
Hopeful
Loving
Motivated
Peaceful
Pleased
Proud
Refreshed
Relaxed
Relieved
Safe
Satisfied
Thankful
Tranquil
Warm

EXCITEMENT + JOY

Adventurous
Alive
Amazed
Courageous
Delighted
Ecstatic
Energetic
Enthusiastic
Excited
Inspired
Invigorated
Joyful/Joyous
Overjoyed
Surprised
Thrilled
Upbeat

FEAR + ANXIETY

Afraid
Alarmed
Anxious
Apprehensive
Bewildered
Cautious
Concerned
Confused
Distraught
Disturbed
Divided
Dubious
Embarrassed
Exposed
Frantic
Impatient
Intimidated
Jittery
Nervous
Panicky
Perplexed
Puzzled
Reluctant
Restless
Rushed
Scared
Shocked
Skeptical
Stressed
Suffocated
Terrified
Threatened
Unsure

OVERWHELM

Activated
Dysregulated
Flooded
Incapable
Off-balance
Over-stimulated
Prodded
Reeling
Shaken
Stirred up
Unsettled

CURIOSITY

Astonished
Awed
Captivated
Curious
Enchanted
Fascinated
Inquisitive
Interested
Intrigued
Lustful
Tempted

HEARTFELT

Compassionate
Empathetic
Hooked
Humbled
Moved
Regret
Remorseful
Sympathetic
Touched

SADNESS + GRIEF

Bad
Crushed
Depressed
Defeated
Despairing
Disappointed
Discouraged
Disheartened
Dismayed
Grief-stricken
Heartbroken
Helpless
Hopeless
Hurt
Lonely
Low
Melancholic
Mournful
Sad
Tearful
Troubled
Weepy

LOW ENERGY + BITTERNESS

Bored
Brittle
Crispy
Depleted
Disinterested
Distracted
Down
Empty
Exasperated
Exhausted
Fatigued
Jaded
Lazy
Low-resourced
Rigid
Running on empty
Sleepy
Sour
Spiritless
Tired
Weary
Worn-out

ANGER + FRUSTRATION

Aggravated
Agitated
Angry
Annoyed
Bothered
Combative
Contempt
Frustrated
Furious
Impatient
Indignant
Judgmental
Livid
Outraged
Rage
Resentful
Short
Tense
Trapped
Unhappy
Upset
Wrathful

DISGUST

Appalled
Disgusted
Grossed out
Nauseated
Repulsed
Sick
Turned off

ATTACHMENT

Abandoned
Alone
Ambivalent
Betrayed
Cheated
Close
Coerced
Connected
Disconnected
Distant
Engaged
Faraway
Forgotten
Guarded
Ignored
Invisible
Isolated
Jealous
Left out
Let down
Longing
Open
Pressured
Pushed out
Stonewalled
Trusting
Unavailable
Violated

REFERENCES

Ainsworth, Mary D. Salter, Mary C. Blehar, Everett Waters, and Sally N. Wall. *Patterns of Attachment: A Psychological Study of the Strange Situation*. New York: Psychology Press, 2015.

Ainsworth, M. D. "The Development of Infant-Mother Attachment." *Review of Child Development Research* 3 (1973): 1–94.

Aldao, Amelia, Susan Nolen-Hoeksema, and Susanne Schwiezer. "Emotion Regulation Strategies Across Psychopathology: A Meta-Analytic Review." *Clinical Psychology Review* 30, no. 2 (2010): 217–37.

Alsubaie, Modi, Rebecca Abbott et al. "Mechanisms of Action in Mindfulness-Based Cognitive Therapy (MBCBT) and Mindfulness-Based Stress Reduction (MBSR) in People with Physical and/or Psychological Conditions: A Systematic Review." *Clinical Psychology Review*, no. 55 (2017): 74–91.

Apostolou, Menelaos, and Andriana Demosthenous. "Why People Forgive Their Intimate Partners' Infidelity: A Taxonomy of Reasons." *Adaptive Human Behavior and Physiology* 7, no. 1 (2021): 54–71.

Apostolou, Menelaos, and Maria Ioannidou. "Strategies of Detecting Infidelity: An Explorative Analysis." *Evolutionary Psychological Science* (2021): 1–10.

Arriaga, X. B., and C. E. Rusbult. "Standing in My Partner's Shoes: Partner Perspective Taking and Reactions to Accommodative Dilemmas." *Personality and Social Psychology Bulletin* 24 (1998): 927–48.

Badenoch, Bonnie. *Being a Brain-Wise Therapist: A Practical Guide to Interpersonal Neurobiology*. New York: Norton, 2008.

Bader, Ellyn, and Peter Pearson. *In Quest of the Mythical Mate: A Developmental Approach to Diagnosis and Treatment in Couples Therapy*. Abingdon, UK: Routledge, 2014.

Baker Miller, Jean. *The Healing Connection: How Women Form Relationships in Therapy and in Life*. Boston, MA: Beacon Press, 1997.

Barstow, Cedar. *Right Use of Power: The Heart of Ethics: A Guide and Resource for Professional Relationships*. Many Realms, 2008.

Bartels, A., and S. Zeki. "The Neural Basis of Romantic Love." *NeuroReport: For Rapid Communication of Neuroscience Research* 11, no. 17 (2000): 3829–34.

Baumeister, Roy F., and Mark R. Leary. "The Need to Belong: Desire for Interpersonal Attachments as a Fundamental Human Motivation." *Psychological Bulletin* 117, no. 3 (1995).

Bawkin, Harry. "Loneliness in Infants." *American Journal of Diseases of Children* 63, no. 1 (1942): 30–40.

Bazzini, D. G., E. R. Stack, et al. "The Effect of Reminiscing About Laughter on Relationship Satisfaction." *Motivation and Emotion* 31 (2007).

Birnbaum, G. E., H. Reis, M. Mikulincer, O. Gillath, and A. Orpaz. "Attachment and Sexual Mating: The Joint Operation of Separate Motivational Systems." In *Handbook of Attachment: Theory, Research, and Clinical Applications, Second Edition*, edited by J. Cassidy and P. A. Shaver, 464–83. New York: Guilford Press, 2016.

Bowlby, John. *Attachment and Loss: Volume One (Attachment)*. New York: Basic Books,1969.

—— *Attachment and Loss: Volume Two (Separation: Anxiety and Anger)*. New York: Basic Books, 1973.

—— *Attachment and Loss: Volume Three (Loss: Sadness and Depression)*. New York: Basic Books, 1980.

—— *The Making and Breaking of Affectional Bonds*. New York: Basic Books, 1980.

—— *A Secure Base: Parent-Child Attachment and Healthy Human Development*.New York: Basic Books, 1969.

Bowlby, John, Margery Fry, and Mary D. Salter Ainsworth. *Child Care and the Growth of Love*. London: Penguin, 1953.

Cacioppo, Stephanie, Haotian Zhou, et al. "You Are in Sync with Me: Neural Correlates of Interpersonal Synchrony with a Partner." *Neuroscience* 277 (2014): 842–58.

Chödrön, Pema. *Welcoming the Unwelcome: Wholehearted Living in a Broken World*. Boulder, CO: Shambhala Publications, 2019.

—— *When Things Fall Apart: Heart Advice for Difficult Times*. Boston, MA: Shambhala Publications, 1996.

Ciurea, Ciprian C. "Unfaithfulness—Cause and/or Effect in Couple Dysfunctionality?" *Scientia Moralitas International Journal of Multidisciplinary Research* 6, no. 1 (2021): 64–78.

Coan, James A., H. S. Schaefer, and R. J. Davidson. "Lending a Hand: Social Regulation of the Neural Response to Threat." (2006). https://doi.org/10.1111/j.1467-9280.2006.01832.x.

Coan, James A., and Davie A. Sbarra. "Social Baseline Theory: The Social Regulation of Risk and Effort." *Current Opinion in Psychology* 1 (2015): 87–91.

Craig, Arthur D. "How Do You Feel? Interoception: The Sense of the Psychological Condition of the Body." *Nature Reviews Neuroscience* 3, no. 8 (2002).

Crenshaw, Kimberlé. *On Intersectionality: Essential Writings*. New York: New Press, 2014.

da Silva, Sérgio P., Charlotte van Oyen Witvliet, and Blake Riek. "Self-Forgiveness and Forgiveness-Seeking in Response to Rumination: Cardiac and Emotional Response of Transgressors." *Journal of Positive Psychology* 12, no. 4 (2017): 362–72.

Damasio, Antonio. *The Strange Order of Things*. New York: Knopf Doubleday, 2017.

Davis, Don E., Man Yee Ho, et al. "Forgiving the Self and Physical and Mental Health Correlates: A Meta-Analytic Review." *Journal of Counseling Psychology* 62, no. 2 (2015).

DeRose, Laurie F., B. R. Johnson, W. Wang, and A. Salazar-Arango. "Couple Religiosity, Male Headship, Intimate Partner Violence, and Infidelity." *Review of Religious Research* (2021): 1–21.

Drigotas, S. M., C. E. Rusbult, and J. Verette. "Level of Commitment, Mutuality of Commitment, and Couple Well-Being." *Personal Relationships*, no. 6 (1999): 839–409.

Drigotas, S. M., and C. E. Rusbult. "Should I Stay or Should I Go? A Dependence Model of Breakups." *Journal of Personality and Social Psychology*, no. 62 (1992): 62–87.

Earley, Jay. *Self-Therapy: A Step-by-Step Guide to Creating Wholeness and Healing Your Inner Child Using IFS, a New Cutting-Edge Psychotherapy.* Pattern System Books, 2009.

Easton, D., and J. W. Hardy. *The Ethical Slut: A Practical Guide to Polyamory, Open Relationships & Other Adventures.* Greenery Press, 1997.

Fan, Rui, Ali Varamesh, et al. "Does Putting Your Emotions into Words Make You Feel Better? Measuring the Minute-Scale Dynamics of Emotions from Online Data." arXiv preprint arXiv: 1807.09725 (2018).

Farrell, D., and C. E. Rusbult. "Exploring the Exit: Voice, Loyalty, and Neglect Typology: The Influence of Job Satisfaction, Quality of Alternatives, and Investment Size." *Employee Responsibility and Rights Journal*, no. 5 (1992): 201–218.

Fern, Jessica. *Polysecure: Attachment, Trauma, and Consensual Nonmonogamy.* Portland, OR: Thorntree Press, 2020.

Finkel, E. G., C. E. Rusbult, M. Kumashiro, and P. A. Hannon. "Dealing with Betrayal in Close Relationships: Does Commitment Promote Forgiveness?" *Journal of Personality and Social Psychology* no. 9 (2002): 956–74. DOI: 10.1037/0022-3514.82.6.956.

Foster, C. A., and C. E. Rusbult. "Injustice and Powerseeking." *Personality and Social Psychology Bulletin*, no. 25 (1999): 834–49. DOI: 10.1177/0146167299025007006.

Friday, Nancy. *Men in Love.* Delta, 1988.

Gaines, S.O., H. T. Reis, S. Summers, C. E. Rusbult, C. L. Cox, M. O. Wexler, W. D. Marelich, and G. J. Kurland. "Impact of Attachment Style on Reactions to Accommodative Dilemmas in Close Relationships." *Personal Relationships*, no. 4 (1997): 93–113.

George, C., N. Kaplan, and M. Main. *Adult Attachment Interview Protocol.* Unpublished manuscript, University of California at Berkeley, 1984.

Gerhardt, Sue. *Why Love Matters: How Affection Shapes a Baby's Brain.* New York: Routledge, 2004.

Glass, Shirley, and J. C. Staeheli. *Not "Just Friends": Rebuilding Trust and Recovering Your Sanity After Infidelity.* New York: Atria, 2002.

Glass, Shirley. "Shattered Vows: Getting Beyond Betrayal." *Psychology Today*, July–August 1998.

Goleman, Daniel. *Emotional Intelligence: Why It Can Matter More than IQ.* New York: Bantam, 2005.

Goodman, Whitney. *Toxic Positivity.* New York: TarcherPerigee, 2022.

Gottman, John. "John Gottman on Trust and Betrayal." *Greater Good Magazine.* October 29, 2011. https://greatergood.berkeley.edu/article/item/john_gottman_on_trust_and_betrayal.

——— *Science of Trust: Emotional Attunement for Couples.* New York: Norton, 2011.

Gottman, John, and Joan DeClaire. *The Relationship Cure: A Five-Step Guide to Strengthening Your Marriage, Family, and Friendships.* New York: Harmony, 2002.

Gottman, John, and Nan Silver. *The Seven Principles for Making Marriage Work: A Practical Guide from the Country's Foremost Relationship Expert.* New York: Harmony, 2015.

——— *What Makes Love Last? How to Build Trust and Avoid Betrayal.* New York: Simon and Schuster, 2012.

Greenspan, Miriam. *Healing Through the Dark Emotions: The Wisdom of Grief, Fear, and Despair.* Boston, MA: Shambhala Publications, 2003.

Hackathorn, Jana, and Brien K. Ashdown. "The Webs We Weave: Predicting Infidelity Motivations and Extradyadic Relationship Satisfaction." *The Journal of Sex Research* 58, no. 2 (2021): 170–82.

Hannon, P. A., C. E. Rusbult, E. J. Finkel, and M. Kashmir. "In the Wake of Betrayal: Amends, Forgiveness, and the Resolution of Betrayal." *Personal Relationships* 12 (253–78). DOI: 10.1111/J.1475-6811.2010.01275.X.

Hannon, P. A., E. J. Finkel, M. Kumarshiro, and Caryl Rusbult. "The Soothing Effects of Forgiveness on Victims' and Perpetrators' Blood Pressure." *Personal Relationships* 19 (2012): 279–89.

Hanson, Rick. *Just One Thing: Developing a Buddha Brain One Simple Practice at a Time.* Oakland, CA: New Harbinger, 2011.

Harris, Nadine Burke. *Toxic Childhood Stress: The Legacy of Early Trauma and How to Heal.* Camden, London: Palgrave Macmillan, 2018.

The Harvard Longevity Study. www.adultdevelopmentstudy.org.

Hendrix, Harville. *Getting the Love You Want: A Guide for Couples.* New York: Henry Holt, 1988.

Holt-Lunstad, Julianne, Timothy B. Smith, and J. Bradley Layton. "Social Relationships and Mortality Risk: A Meta-Analytic Review." *Public Library of Science Medicine.*

hooks, bell. *All About Love.* New York: HarperCollins, 2000.

Iacoboni, Marco. "Imitation, Empathy, and Mirror Neurons." *Annual Review of Psychology,* 60 (2009) 653-70.

Johnson, Sue. *Hold Me Tight: Seven Conversations for a Lifetime of Love.* New York: Little, Brown, 2008.

——— *Love Sense: The Revolutionary New Science of Romantic Relationships.* New York: Little, Brown, 2013.

Joseph, S. "Growth Following Adversity: Positive Psychological Perspectives on Posttraumatic Stress." *Psihologijske Teme* 18, no. 2 (2009): 335–44.

Kubacka, K. E., C. Finkenauer, C. E. Rusbult, and L. Keijsers. "Maintaining Closer Relationships: Gratitude as a Motivator and Detector of Maintenance Behavior." *Personality and Social Psychology Bulletin* 37 (2011): 1362–75. DOI: 10.1177/0146167211412196.

Kumashiro, M., C. E. Rusbult, and E. J. Finkel. "Navigating Personal and Relational Concerns: The Quest for Equilibrium." *Journal of Personality and Social Psychology* 95 (2008): 94–110.

——— "Self-Respect and Pro-Relationship Behavior in Marital Relationships." *Journal of Personality* no. 70 (2002): 1009–49.

Lambert, Nathaniel M., Frank D. Fincham, and Tyler F. Stillman. "Gratitude and Depressive Symptoms: The Role of Positive Reframing and Positive Emotion." *Cognition and Emotion* 26, no. 4 (2012): 615–33.

Levine, Amir, and Rachel Heller. *Attached: The New Science of Adult Attachment and How It Can Help You Find—and Keep—Love.* New York: TarcherPerigee, 2012.

Levine, E. C., C. Herbenick, and O. Martinez. "Open Relationships, Nonconsensual Nonmonogamy, and Monogamy Among U.S. Adults: Findings from the 2012 National Survey of Sexual Health and Behavior." *Archives of Sexual Behavior* 47, no. 5 (2018): 1439–1450.

Levine, Peter. *Healing Trauma: A Pioneering Program for Restoring the Wisdom of Your Body.* Boulder, CO: Sounds True, 2008.

——— *In an Unspoken Voice: How the Body Releases Trauma and Restores Goodness.* Berkeley, CA: North Atlantic Books, 2010.

Luchies, L. B., J. Wiselquist, C. E. Rusbult, M. Kumashiro, P. W. Eastwick, M. K. Coolsen, and E. J. Finkel. "Trust and Biased Memory of Transgressions in Romantic Relationships." *Journal of Personality and Social Psychology* 104 (2013): 673–94.

Macaskill, Ann. "Differentiating Dispositional Self-Forgiveness from Other-Forgiveness: Associations with Mental Health and Life Satisfaction." *Journal of Social and Clinical Psychology* 31, no. 1 (2012): 28–50.

MacBeth, Angus, and Andrew Gumley. "Exploring Compassion: A Meta-Analysis of the Association Between Self-Compassion and Psychopathology." *Clinical Psychology Review* 32, no. 6 (2012): 545–52.

Main, Mary, N. Kaplan, and J. Cassidy. "Security in Infancy, Childhood and Adulthood: A Move to the Level of Representation." In *Growing Points of Attachment Theory and Research*, edited by I. Bretherton and E. Waters. Monographs of the Society for Research in Child Development, 50 (1985), Serial No. 209., 66–104.

Mark, K. P., L. M. Vowels, and S. H. Murray. "The Impact of Attachment Style on Sexual Satisfaction and Sexual Desire in a Sexually Diverse Sample." *Journal of Sex and Marital Therapy* 44, no. 5 (2018): 450–458.

Maté, Gabor. *In the Realm of Hungry Ghosts: Close Encounters with Addiction.* Berkeley, CA: North Atlantic Books, 2010.

——— *When the Body Says No: The Hidden Cost of Stress.* Toronto: Vintage Canada, 2004.

McRae, Kateri, and Iris B. Mauss. "Increasing Positive Emotion in Negative Contexts: Emotional Consequences, Neural Correlates, and Implications for Resilience." *Positive Neuroscience* (2016): 159–174.

Meenadchi. *Decolonizing Non-Violent Communication*. Los Angeles: CO-COnspirator Press, Women's Center for Creative Work, 2019.

Meyer, Pamela. *Liespotting: Proven Techniques to Detect Deception*. New York: St. Martin's Press, 2010.

Miller, William R., and Stephen Rollnick. *Motivational Interviewing: Helping People Change*. New York: Guilford Press, 2012.

Mitchell, Erika., A.Wittenborn, T. M. Timm, and A. J. Blow. "Affair Recovery: Exploring Similarities and Differences of Injured and Involved Partners." *Journal of Marital and Family Therapy* (2021).

Moors, A. C., W. S. Ryan, and W. J. Chopik. "Multiple Loves: The Effects of Attachment with Multiple Concurrent Romantic Partners on Relational Functioning." *Personality and Individual Differences* 147 (2019): 102–110.

Nagoski, Amelia and Emily. *Burnout: The Secret to Unlocking the Stress Cycle*. New York: Ballantine Books, 2019.

Nagoski, Emily. *Come As You Are: The Surprising New Science That Will Transform Your Sex Life*. New York,: Simon and Schuster, 2015.

Navarra, Robert. "The Path to Infidelity: What Gottman Research Tells Us." drrobertnavarra.com/gottman-research-on-infidelity.

Neff, Kristin D., and Christopher K. Germer. "A Pilot Study and Randomized Controlled Trial of the Mindful Self-Compassion Program." *Journal of Clinical Psychology* 69, no. 1 (2013): 28–44.

Neff, Kristin. *Fierce Self-Compassion: How Women Can Harness Kindness to Speak Up, Claim Their Power, and Thrive*. New York: HarperCollins, 2021.

——— *Self-Compassion: The Proven Power of Being Kind to Yourself*. New York: HarperCollins, 2011.

Odebode, A. A., J. F. James, K. A. Adegunku, and J. Julia. "Aftermaths of Infidelity as Expressed by Literate Working Class Women in Lagos State, Nigeria." *Journal of Nusantara Studies* (2021): 41–57.

Ogden, Pat, and Janina Fisher. *Sensorimotor Psychotherapy: Interventions for Trauma and Attachment*. New York: Norton, 2015.

Park, Crystal L. "The Meaning Making Model: A Framework for Understanding Meaning, Spirituality, and Stress-Related Growth in Health Psychology." *European Health Psychologist* 15, no. 2 (2013): 40–47.

Perel, Esther. *Mating in Captivity: Unlocking Erotic Intelligence*. New York: HarperCollins, 2006.

——— *The State of Affairs: Rethinking Infidelity*. New York: HarperCollins, 2017.

Poole-Heller, Diane. *The Power of Attachment: How to Create Deep and Lasting Intimate Relationships*. Boulder, CO: Sounds True, 2019.

Pramudito, A. A., and W. M. Minza. "The Dynamics of Rebuilding Trust and Trustworthiness in Marital Relationship Post Infidelity Disclosure." *Journal Psikologi* 48, no. 2 (2021): 16–30.

Purvanova, Radostina, K., and John P. Muros. "Gender Differences in Burnout: A Meta-Analysis." *Journal of Vocational Behavior* 77, no. 2 (2010): 168–185.

Raden, Aja. *The Truth About Lies: The Illusion of Honesty and The Evolution of Deceit.* New York: St. Martin's Press, 2021.

Raftar Aliabadi, Mohammad R., and Hossein Shareh. "Mindfulness-Based Schema Therapy and Forgiveness Therapy Among Women Affected by Infidelity: A Randomized Clinical Trial." *Psychotherapy Research* (2021): 1–13.

Real, Terrence. *The New Rules of Marriage: What You Need to Know to Make Love Work.* New York: Ballantine Books, 2008.

Rezamahalleh, Maryam S. "Predicting Attitudes Toward Marital Infidelity Based on Attachment and Perfectionism Styles." *Journal of Modern Psychology* 1, no. 1 (2021): 51–64.

Robles, Theodore F., Richard B. Slatcher, et al. "Marital Quality and Health: A Meta-Analytic Review." *Psychological Bulletin* 140, no. 1 (2014): 140–87.

Rothschild, Babette. *The Body Remembers: The Psychophysiology of Trauma and Trauma Treatment.* New York: Norton, 2000.

——— *8 Keys to Safe Trauma Recovery: Take-Charge Strategies to Empower Your Healing.* New York: Norton, 2010.

Rothstein, Nina J., D. H. Connolly, E. J. de Visser, and E. Phillips. "Perceptions of Infidelity with Sex Robots." *Proceedings of the 2021 ACM/IEEE International Conference of Human-Robot Interaction* (2021): 129–139.

Rusbult, C. E., I. M. Zembrodt, and L. K. Gunn. "Exit, Voice, Loyalty, and Neglect: Responses to Dissatisfaction in Romantic Involvements." *Journal of Personality and Social Psychology* 43 (1982): 1230–42. DOI: 10.1037/0022-3514.43.6.1230.

Rusbult, C. E., J. M. Martz, and C. R. Agnew. "The Investment Model Scale: Measuring Commitment Level, Satisfaction Level, Quality of Alternatives, and Investment Size." *Personal Relationships* 5 (1998): 357–391. https://doi.org/10.1111/j.1475-6811.1998.tb00177.x.

Rusbult, C. E., P. A. Van Lange, T. Wildschut, N. A. Yovetich, and J. Verette. "Perceived Superiority in Closer Relationships: Why It Exists and Persists." *Journal of Personality and Social Psychology* 79 (2000): 521–45. DOI: 10.1037/0022-3514.79.4.521.

Rusbult, Caryl E., C. R. Agnew, and X. B. Arriaga. "The Investment Model of Commitment Processes." *Handbook of Theories of Social Psychology* (2012): 218–231. DOI: 10.4135/97814462492222.n37.

Saad, Layla. *Me and White Supremacy: Combat Racism, Change the World, and Become a Good Ancestor.* Naperville, IL: Sourcebooks, 2020.

Sakman, E., B. Urganci, and B. Sevi. "Your Cheating Heart Is Just Afraid of Ending Up Alone: Fear of Being Single Mediates the Relationship Between Attachment Anxiety and Infidelity." *Personality and Individual Differences* 168 (2021): 110366.

Sapolsky, Robert. *Behave: The Biology of Humans at Our Best and Worst.* New York: Penguin Books, 2018.

Schwartz, Richard. *Internal Family Systems Therapy.* New York: Guilford Press, 1997.

Selterman, D., J. R. Garcia, and I. Tsapelas. "What Do People Do, Say, and Feel When They Have Affairs? Associations Between Extradyadic Infidelity Motives with Behavioral, Emotional, and Sexual Outcomes." *Journal of Sex and Marital Therapy* 47, no. 3 (2021): 238–52.

Semenyna, Scott W., F. R. Gomez Jimenez, and P. L. Vasey. "Women's Reaction to Opposite- and Same-Sex Infidelity in Three Cultures." *Human Nature* 32, no. 2 (2021): 450–69.

Sharabie, Liesel L., M. Uhlich, C. Alexopoulos, and E. Timmermans. "Exploring Links Between Online Infidelity, Mate Poaching Intentions, and the Likelihood of Meeting Offline." *Cyberpsychology, Behavior, and Social Networking* 24, no. 7 (2021): 450–56.

Siegel, Daniel. *The Developing Mind: How Relationships and the Brain Interact to Shape Who We Are.* New York: Guilford Press, 2001.

Simpson, J. A., and J. Belsky. "Attachment Theory within a Modern Evolutionary Framework." In *Handbook of Attachment: Theory, Research, and Clinical Applications, Third Edition,* edited by Jude Cassidy and Phillip R. Shaver. New York: Guilford Press, 2018.

St. David, Gena. "Reconciling Counselors' Christian Beliefs and Lesbian, Gay, Bisexual, and Transgender Affirmation: A Grounded Theory." *Counseling and Values* 63, Issue 1 (2018). DOI: 10.1002/cvj.12076.

Steger, Michael F. "Experiencing Meaning in Life." In *The Human Quest for Meaning: Theories, Research, and Applications.* New York: Routledge, 2012.

Tafoya, M., and B. Spitzberg. "The Dark Side of Infidelity: Its Nature, Prevalence and Communicative Functions." In *The Dark Side of Interpersonal Communication,* edited by B. Spitzberg and W. Cupach, 211–52. New York: Routledge, 2009.

Taormino, Tristan. *Opening Up: A Guide to Creating and Sustaining Open Relationships.* San Francisco, CA: Cleis Press, 2008.

Tatkin, Stan. *We Do: Saying Yes to a Relationship of Depth, True Connection, and Enduring Love.* Boulder, CO: Sounds True, 2018.

——— *Wired for Dating: How Understanding Neurobiology and Attachment Style Can Help You and Your Ideal Mate.* Oakland, CA: New Harbinger, 2016.

——— *Wired for Love: How Understanding Your Partner's Brain and Attachment Style Can Help You Defuse Conflict and Build a Safe Relationship.* Oakland, CA: New Harbinger, 2012.

——— "Ten Commandments for a Secure-Functioning Relationship." In *For Couples: Ten Commandments for Every Aspect of Your Relationship Journey,* edited by J. K. Zeig and T. Kulbatski, 2011.

Tawwab, Nedra. *Set Boundaries, Find Peace: A Guide to Reclaiming Yourself.* New York: TarcherPerigee, 2021.

Taylor, Sonya Renee. *The Body Is Not an Apology: The Power of Radical Self-Love.* Berrett-Koehler, 2018.

Toepfer, Steven M., K. Chichy, and P. Peters. "Letters of Gratitude: Further Evidence for Author Benefits." *Journal of Happiness Studies* 13, no. 1 (2012): 187–201.

Torre, J. B., and M. D. Lieberman. "Putting Feelings into Words: Affect Labeling as Implicit Emotion Regulation." *Emotion Review* 10, no. 2 (2018): 116–24.

Tronick, Edward. *Babies as People*. New York: Collier Books, 1980.

Tyler, J. M., and K. C. Burns. "After Depletion: The Replenishment of the Self's Regulatory Resources." *Self and Identity* 7, no. 3 (2008): 305–21.

Valdesolo, P., J. Ouyand, and D. De Steno. "The Rhythm of Joint Action: Synchrony Promotes Cooperative Ability." *Journal of Experimental Social Psychology* 46, no. 4 (July 2010): 693–95.

Vangelisti, A. L., and M. Gerstenberger. "Communication and Marital Infidelity." In *The State of Affairs: Explorations in Infidelity and Commitment*, edited by J. Duncombe, K. Harrison, G. Allen, and D. Marsden. Mahwah, NJ: Lawrence Erlbaum, 2004.

Van Lange, P. A., and Caryl E. Rusbult. *Interdependence Theory Handbook of Theories of Social Psychology*, 251–272. DOI: 10.4135/9781446249222.n39.

Van Lange, P. A., C. E. Rusbult, S. M. Drigotas, X. B. Arriaga, B. S. Witcher, and C. L. Cox. "Willingness to Sacrifice in Close Relationships." *Journal of Personality and Social Psychology*, no. 72 (1997): 1373–95. DOI: 10.1037/0022-3514.72.6.1373.

Wallin, David. *Attachment in Psychotherapy*. New York: Guilford Press, 2015.

Warach, Benjamin, and Lawrence Josephs. "The Aftershocks of Infidelity: A Review of Infidelity-Based Attachment Trauma." *Sexual and Relationship Therapy* 36, no. 1 (2021): 68–90.

Wilkinson, Dulce E., and William L. Dunlop. "Both Sides of the Story: Narratives of Romantic Infidelity." *Personal Relationships* 28, no. 1 (2021): 121–47.

Wiselquist, J., C. E. Rusbult, C. A. Foster, and C. R. Agnew. "Commitment, Pro-Relationship Behavior, and Trust in Close Relationships." *Journal of Personality and Social Psychology*, no. 77 (1999): 942–66.

Witvliet, C. V. O., A. J. Hofelich Mohr, et al. "Transforming or Restraining Rumination: The Impact of Compassionate Reappraisal versus Emotion Suppression on Empathy, Forgiveness, and Affective Psychophysiology." *Journal of Positive Psychology* 10 (2015): 248–61.

Zeifman, D., and C. Hazan. "Pair Bonds as Attachments: Reevaluating the Evidence." In *The Handbook of Attachment: Theory, Research, and Clinical Applications*, edited by J. Cassidy and P. R. Shaver, 436–54. New York: Guilford Press, 2018.

INDEX

Page numbers in **bold** indicate tables or figures.

ABOUT THE AUTHOR

 **Morgan Johnson, MA** is a licensed professional counselor (LPC), trust-recovery specialist, speaker, and author living in Austin, Texas. She received a BA in psychology from Wake Forest University and completed an MA in counseling at St. Edward's University. She experiences a sense of purpose through helping people connect with themselves and others in her practice as well as through her writing. When she isn't working, Morgan can be found outside enjoying the Texas sunshine with Leo the dog or tucked away with a book and Bruce the cat. You can connect with Morgan on social media @ConnectWithMorganJohnson.

Hi there,

We hope *Rebuilding Trust* helped you. If you have any questions or concerns about your book, or have received a damaged copy, please contact customerservice@penguinrandomhouse.com. We're here and happy to help.

Also, please consider writing a review on your favorite retailer's website to let others know what you thought of the book!

Sincerely,
The Zeitgeist Team